# TAROT & TEQUILA

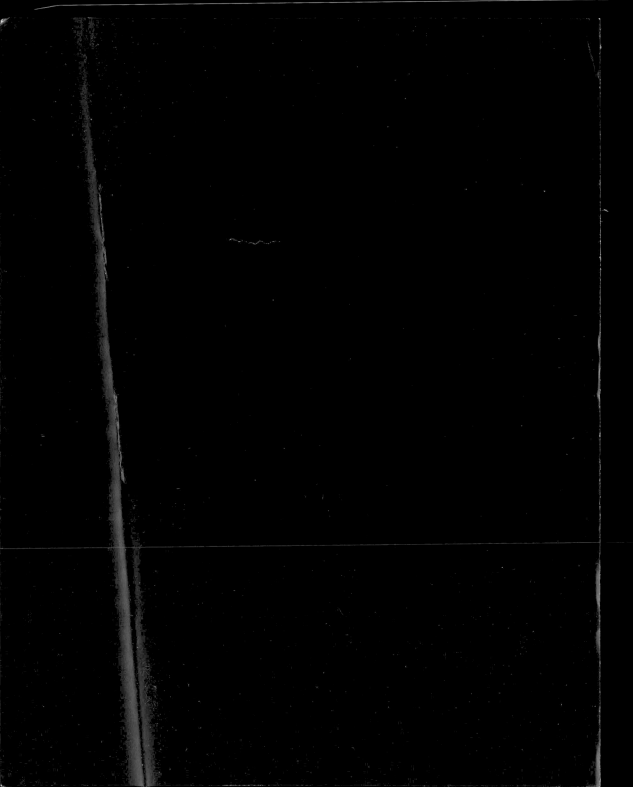

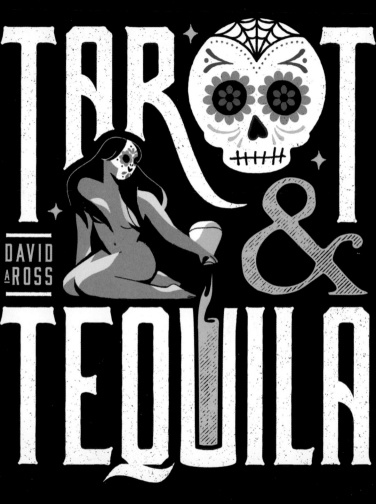

A TAROT GUIDE with COCKTAILS

# TAROT & TEQUILA

DAVID A ROSS

and OTHER SPIRITS

TILLER PRESS

New York   London   Toronto   Sydney   New Delhi

TILLER PRESS

An Imprint of Simon & Schuster, Inc.
1230 Avenue of the Americas
New York, NY 10020

First Tiller Press hardcover edition July 2021

TILLER PRESS and colophon are trademarks of Simon & Schuster, Inc.

For information about special discounts for bulk purchases, please contact
Simon & Schuster Special Sales at 1-866-506-1949 or business@simonandschuster.com.

The Simon & Schuster Speakers Bureau can bring authors to your live event.
For more information or to book an event, contact the Simon & Schuster Speakers
Bureau at 1-866-248-3049 or visit our website at www.simonspeakers.com.

Interior design by Patrick Sullivan and Jennifer Chung
Illustrations by Carolina Martínez
Skull and Shot Glass Icons by Shutterstock

Manufactured in China

3  5  7  9  10  8  6  4  2

Library of Congress Cataloging-in-Publication Data
Names: Ross, David, 1972– author.
Title: Tarot & tequila : a tarot guide with cocktails / by David Ross. Description:
New York : Tiller Press, 2021. | Includes index. Identifiers: LCCN 2020041376 (print) |
LCCN 2020041377 (ebook) | ISBN 9781982169381 (hardcover) |
ISBN 9781982169411 (ebook) | Subjects: LCSH: Tarot. | Tequila. | Cocktails. |
Classification: LCC BF1879.T2 R68 2021 (print) |
LCC BF1879.T2 (ebook) | DDC 133.3/2424—dc23
LC record available at https://lccn.loc.gov/2020041376
LC ebook record available at https://lccn.loc.gov/2020041377

ISBN 978-1-9821-6938-1
ISBN 978-1-9821-6941-1 (ebook)

*I'd like to dedicate this book
to all my fellow light bringers.
Keep bringing the light!*

# CONTENTS

# INTRODUCTION

*I'd like to raise a glass of tequila in honor of where I grew up.*

Here's to the Jersey Shore!

I grew up in a very close yet religiously diverse family in Middletown, New Jersey. My grandmother on my mother's side came to the United States when she was seventeen, after meeting my grandfather in Cuba during World War II. My grandmother was raised Catholic and converted to Judaism later in life for her husband, and, for some unknown reason, their two children didn't gravitate toward any one religion, and of course that trickled down to me. Growing up with no particular religion allowed me to take my time and find my own path.

I went to college at Roger Williams University in Rhode Island. I majored in communication while taking many courses in journalism as well. I aspired to be a rock and roll journalist. It was during those social years that I fell in love with astrology. It was soon after college that astrology led me to reading tarot cards, which I believe are spiritually and functionally linked. I was the guy who'd say, "What's your sign?" as a pickup line and was genuinely interested in the answer.

I married my wife, Alison, in 2001, around the same time I got my start in the pharmaceutical industry. Alison was raised Presbyterian, and even though we baptized our children in this religion, I found myself taking a more spiritual journey, one that was more personal.

As a medical sales representative, I quickly learned that the people I worked with were genuinely interested in my reading tarot cards. No matter who it was—doctors, nurses, office managers, medical assistants—just about anyone wanted their cards read. When I obliged, I found that by reading a person's cards we became somehow connected. People surprisingly opened up to me and we would have these intense emotional conversations that meant more to me than I would have ever expected.

I just want to be clear, I'm not psychic nor do I see spirits or claim to be something I am not. I see myself as an empath, which enables me to form strong, meaningful connections with the people I read for. For me, tarot cards are a very useful tool that can be used to help people work through problems in their lives. Whether it be through a tarot reading or by meditating on the cards for yourself, there are many lessons that can be learned through their symbolism and interpretations. Personally, tarot helps me navigate through the issues that arise in my day-to-day life. Still to this day, I pull a tarot card each morning and keep it with me throughout the day. Whether it's on my car's dashboard or on a shelf in my office, I can meditate on its personal messages and gain further insight to what the card is telling me.

So, after twenty-five years of reading tarot cards, I finally decided to make it an actual business. And Tarot and Tequila was born. Where does tequila fit in, you may wonder? It's actually quite simple. I have a love for both tequila and tarot, so in my eyes they are perfectly paired.

Tarot and Tequila is a tarot reading business where I not only read cards at bars and restaurants, but for private corporate functions as well. My vision of Tarot and Tequila, however, is more than just tarot cards and tequila drinks. It's really a movement of both positivity and empowerment. And with this book, I am thrilled to offer my unique style of tarot, along with another one of my passions, in a crossover attempt to bring much happiness and insight into a sometimes upside-down world.

## FINDING TAROT

Let me begin by explaining my journey into the mystery of tarot. I wish I could tell you that it was a calling from my early childhood, but if I'm being completely honest, it was an impulse buy. How awesome would it be if could start my story off with how I was born with second sight or some kind of wizard's mark on my forehead? That I'm actually the seventh son of a seventh son and spent my life as a Romani fortune-teller in a traveling carnival? But, alas, I cannot say any of those things. My introduction to tarot started very ordinarily.

Let's journey back to 1995. Can you recall what you were doing and where you were heading that year? I had recently graduated college and was invited to a friend's wedding in Santa Fe. I'd never been there and thought it might be a fun adventure.

The few days I spent in New Mexico were inspirational. New Mexico was so unlike New Jersey in every way possible, and it took some time getting used to. The altitude difference alone is a shock if you aren't prepared for it. Huffing and puffing up a flight of stairs at twenty-three years of age was daunting, and my first reaction was that I definitely needed to exercise more.

My hotel was surrounded by stunning mountain views. The Santa Fe square was bustling with activity. Hippies were playing Hacky Sack on the grass while Native

Americans sold their silver-and-turquoise jewelry on handwoven blankets. I felt like I was back in time and experienced an odd connection to a place I'd only seen in pictures before. I was in my early twenties, still impressionable, still gravitating toward stores that sold childlike things. I made my way to a toy store, poking around, looking for a Santa Fe keepsake. The store wasn't very large, and thinking that I had seen everything, I started to make my exit when, as I walked past the cash register, something caught my eye. I noticed a glass bowl filled with small decks of cards. I stopped, reached in, and grabbed one. How fun! The world's smallest deck of tarot cards complete with seventy-eight individually painted cards in a pack. I don't know why but I had to have one.

If you look back upon your life and recall how many hobbies or projects you've started but never completed, what would your number be? Mine would be astronomical. I tried a stint in advertising; I took courses in American Sign Language when I thought I wanted to be a speech pathologist; and straight out of college, as I mentioned, I wanted to be a rock and roll journalist.

I never imagined a tiny deck of tarot cards would lead to a lifetime passion. Over twenty years later, the number of tarot books I own fills several bookshelves. Eventually I got to the point where I stopped buying them. Many included the same content—pictures of the traditional Rider-Waite Tarot Deck accompa-

Remember these important pieces of advice when reading for others:

**1.** If you are new to tarot, start with a simple three-card spread; reading left to right, the cards represent your past, present, and future.

**2.** I personally use the ten-card Celtic Cross spread, for which you can find myriad variations online.

**3.** Pay attention to any overlapping themes in the reading. Are there more cups than any other suit? Chances are we're in the middle of a love reading.

**4.** Utilize clarifying cards when you aren't sure. A clarifying card is when you pick another card to help with the meaning of the first. It can make a card better or it can make it worse, or it can make you go *hmmm*.

nied by a description of each card and explanations of what the cards meant in both upright and reversed positions. Some include examples of tarot card spreads and actual readings based off those spreads. I eventually realized that I was buying essentially the same book with some small variations and differences.

Before my personal relationship with tarot evolved to where it is today, I'll admit that at times I was a little intimidated. There are people who associate tarot with the occult and have painted a very negative view of the cards. When I first started, I even wondered, "Are these dark arts that I'm practicing?" There have been times when I would put down my cards after a reading that was too spot-on, and I was a little freaked out. Luckily, those days are behind me and my current outlook on tarot is, as I've said, one of positivity and empowerment!

Both of these motivations are at the core of *Tarot & Tequila*! It's the sun on your face or the hand gently pressed on your back . . . it's the reassurance you look toward when times seem darkest. It's a reinforcing message that you are capable of anything you put your mind to. It celebrates that we are all the same, no matter how different we may be. Readers will understand and relate to tarot cards in a new, refreshing way. Instead of the same old definitions and interpretations of tarot cards that you may be used to seeing, *Tarot & Tequila* connects the cards to everyday situations that affect us all.

This is where the tequila comes in. Tarot and tequila, when paired together, evoke great personal joy! When I started Tarot and Tequila as a small business, I hosted nights at local bars and restaurants in hopes of introducing tarot cards to a different audience of people. I copromoted with tequila marketers, and we created tequila-based mixed drinks, naming them after tarot cards. That first event turned out to be a great success! I ended up doing readings for three hours straight, barely having a moment to relax. Pairing mixed drinks with tarot cards went over really well and our success grew. But by far the best part of Tarot and Tequila nights are the connections I make with the people for whom I do readings. So many of us are looking for answers and reassurances, and I am pleased to be able to bring some light to people who may be dealing with some darkness in their lives.

*Tarot & Tequila* combines these two things I'm passionate about in hopes of being a source of self-help and bringing simple happiness to those who may need it. My card interpretations will help you relate these gorgeously illustrated card representations to everyday situations and scenarios. You'll be learning to read tarot cards without even knowing you're doing it. The days of memorization are over! Let these stunning sugar skull cards speak to you however they speak to you. Let them have their own unique voice intertwined with your own unique intuition. (While any tarot deck you have on hand can work with this book, if the sugar skull imagery resonates strongly with you, you'll be able to get this special set of cards in addition to this book.)

And let my mystical pairing sections show you a deeper connection between a card and its paired drink. Within these paragraphs I've incorporated little rituals to help you manifest the powerful aspects of the cards you would like to embody. Making a cocktail can be a ritual in and of itself; with my mystical pairings, we are really ritualizing it with other components and words of affirmation.

Let's together raise our glasses and say, "Tarot and tequila!"

I fell in love with sugar skulls later in life. My dad moved out to Arizona and my family periodically visited him. I've always been drawn to that part of the country. Visiting places like Sedona and Old Town Scottsdale (besides the natural beauty of the landscape), I became fascinated with all the beautifully designed sugar skulls being sold and on display. Sugar skulls are traditionally used during Día de los Muertos to decorate altars and are made from granulated sugar.

# TOOLS *of the* TRADE

**W**hether you're a mixologist or a Wiccan, you will need the proper items to help correctly make your cocktails/potions. It doesn't matter if you're behind a bar or in front of your cauldron, if you need it, it's here.

---

**COCKTAIL STRAINER.** You must treat your altar with care. What will your sisters think if you start your drinking ritual with sticky glasses and candles? Unless flies are part of the ritual, you don't want them hovering about.

**MUDDLER.** Yes, your mortar and pestle will work just as well. I won't ask you to buy a stainless-steel one when your wooden go-to is sitting right there. Just clean it first!

**JIGGER/DOUBLE JIGGER.** Making these magical concoctions takes precise measuring. Five ounces off in any particular way could cause a minor rift in the universe. You wouldn't want to be in the process of making a delicious elixir and then have it suddenly disappear, would you?

**CITRUS JUICER.** You don't need a fancy electric juicer that can also walk your snake for you. A simple manual one will do just fine.

**BARSPOON/MIXING SPOON.** Many of these potions require a precise number of stirs. I know you have a magic wand or sacred stick that is waterproof, but I would never ask you to use that. A simple long spoon will do just fine.

**CUTTING BOARDS AND DAGGERS.** Many of these beverages require fruit that needs cutting, like lemons, limes, and other such citrusy things. You can use your sacrificial dagger, but a paring knife will also do the trick.

**SHAKER.** When a cocktail is not being stirred, it's most likely being shaken. Remember when we talked about the proper amount of each ingredient? You'll know what I'm talking about if you've measured incorrectly and start shaking. Tick . . . Tick . . . BOOM!

**MIXING CHALICE.** Any old glass will do, of course. You do want one large enough, though, to fit all of those pesky ingredients. You wouldn't want any climbing out!

**MEASURING CUPS.** These are mostly used for making your simple sugar recipes. You can use them in place of your jiggers, but there's no telling what could magically happen if you do that. You'll be hammered!

**CITRUS ZESTER.** Making the most from your ingredients is of the utmost importance. Adding zest to your elixir brings about a wonderful scent component. The magical oils touching your lips heightens the overall experience as well.

**SAUCEPAN/CAULDRON.** When making your homemade simple sugar potions, you will need that water nice and bubbly. Most of the time simple sugar is just water, sugar, and whatever component you wish to add. Leave the little winged creatures alone and remember your newts need both eyes, please.

**MASON JARS.** I know you have jars lying around your lair. Where do you keep all your "spices"? Surely not in a cupboard or drawer.

**SUGAR.** I know you're as sweet as can be already. Nonetheless, you'll need a lot of these white granules in bulk to make these cocktails. Show everyone what a "sugar mouth" you are!

**FRUITS, FLAVORS, LEAVES, FLOWERS, AND ALL OTHER TASTY THINGS.** Rose petals, mint leaves, peppermint, lotus tea, honey, snakeskin, bat wool, spider webs. Just kidding about the last three. You get the point.

**CANDLES.** Because every good "bartender" needs candles, right?

**CRYSTALS.** I'm not judging, but you know all those pretty, sparkly stones on your window shelves and tables? The ones that make your backyard shine and give it so much character? The ones your partner says are taking over the entire house and "becoming a hoarding problem"? Yes! Those. I know you have them, so let's use them.

**CHARGED CRYSTALS.** Take your quartz crystals (azurite, tiger's eye, jade, moonstone, and whatever other crystals you intend on using) and place them in moonlight or sunlight. You can set your stones outside before bed and bring them in before noon if you like, for ten to twelve hours. Other charging methods include a sea salt bath for a few hours to a few days, and sage will also work (allow the smoke to envelop the stones for thirty seconds).

**A FAMILIAR.** Whether it be a loyal canine or an observant owl, everyone needs a sidekick.

**NOTE:** You will have leftover simple syrups if you make the cocktails as directed. Any leftover syrups are also great as a sweetener to an iced tea or drizzled over ice cream!

# The MAJOR ARCANA

## x x x

*What the margarita is the Major Arcana?*

Simply put, the Major Arcana need to have exclamation points after them. If you were making a cocktail, the Major Arcana would be the tequilas, vodkas, gins, and bourbons. Traditionally, the term "Major Arcana" refers to the Fool's quest for enlightenment. The Fool is number zero of the twenty-two Major Arcana cards, and 1 through 21 show his journey and how it can relate to our own. I'm talking about big events like birth, death, milestones, landmarks, all of our major life experiences, and the lessons we treasure and fear in order to grow and learn. The Major Arcana should never be taken lightly, especially when there is an abundance of them in your reading. If you get more than three in a ten-card spread, the universe is really trying to tell you something—and you should listen!

# 0        *The* **FOOL**

## BASIC DEFINITION

Who doesn't like fresh starts and new beginnings? The Fool is not being foolish. They're on a new adventure, and it's part of their soul's progress toward enlightenment. When you are filled with a universal knowledge that you are doing exactly what you need to and at exactly the right time, that's the Fool's energy. Your friends and family may think you're walking off a cliff toward the unknown and uncertainty, but you instinctively know you are making the right decision. Sometimes you have to step outside the box and embrace your inner child.

## *Reversed* BASIC DEFINITION

While the Fool talks about being a free spirit and following your instincts because you know it's the right thing to do, the Fool Reversed wants you to check with friends before making decisions. It could be that your course of action is a bit naïve and even foolish. You may be making impulsive or rash decisions. There is also the fear of believing everything you are told, so just because you are innocent and spontaneous, it doesn't mean you have to be gullible, too.

## TEQUILA DEFINITION

Just get in your car and drive. Who says you need a plan? Your favorite band is playing at a local club and, honestly, you don't care who's going or how you're getting home. All you know is that you're going to have an amazing night, with or without your friends. You won't have a problem making new friends or striking up conversations with like-minded people. You have that optimism and innocence people find infectious; you'll be just fine.

## *Reversed* TEQUILA DEFINITION

Listen, I know you want to have a good time, but maybe doing a row of shots to kick off your night might not be the smartest idea. Please don't think driving home after you've clearly had way too many drinks is the right thing to do either. Why don't you call an Uber and let someone else make the important decisions for you? Nobody wants to deal with a fool, and especially a drunk fool, making poor reckless choices.

# The
# MYSTICAL PAIRING

*Does the idea of something new excite you? What if you reinvented a classic? Sounds exciting to me! Picture a new beginning stemming from something that has long been a source of tradition. It's like being awakened by a new sound or seeing your lover of many years in a brand-new, innocent way.*

*I'm speaking about the traditional Negroni. On its own, it's a delicious beverage; however, the Fool doesn't stand for tradition. He loves trying new things. By replacing the gin and sweet vermouth with espresso-infused tequila and Fonseca Ruby Port, it would seem like a brand-new drink while being prepared in the very same classical way.*

*When you are about to undertake something new and you can feel the Fool's energy swimming around you, make this drink and say, "I embrace all new things!*

*"I am the beginning and I am awake!"*

*Serve in* ⟍ / *a double rocks glass*

# *The* FOOL COCKTAIL

1 1/2 OUNCES ESPRESSO-INFUSED AÑEJO TEQUILA

1 1/2 OUNCES CAMPARI

1 1/2 OUNCES FONSECA RUBY PORT

ZEST OF 1 LEMON

✦

*Pour equal parts of all of the ingredients into a mixing glass with ice and stir. Strain into a double rocks glass with one large ice cube. Garnish with the lemon zest.*

The MAGICIAN

# 1     *The* MAGICIAN

✳✳✳✳✳✳✳✳✳✳✳✳✳✳✳✳✳✳✳✳✳✳✳✳✳✳✳✳✳✳✳✳

## BASIC DEFINITION

The Magician reminds us how magical we truly are! We sometimes forget that we have everything we need already within us to manifest our true potential. Power, skill, and mastery are all a part of us already. We just need to direct that energy and make it happen. You're ready. It's time to show the world your full potential. Don't make them wait a second longer to see the real you.

## *Reversed* BASIC DEFINITION

Why are you not utilizing the potential you clearly have? Everyone can see your talent is being wasted. The Magician Reversed tells us to rediscover your muse! Look for inspiration to remove that creative block and show the world that you can do more than talk the talk.

## TEQUILA DEFINITION

Have you ever seen that man or woman at a party or bar who knows they have their shit together? Walking confidently up to their blind date and starting up a conversation like it was nothing at all? Casually ordering the beautiful soul at the other end of the bar a drink? So smooth in their gestures and attitude. They arrive and exit every party or function on their own terms, completely in control of the situation they've created.

## *Reversed* TEQUILA DEFINITION

So you were dragged out tonight by your friends but you really aren't feeling it? Tonight might be the night you sit back and chill. Let your friends do the talking and decision-making because on this night you're a little too apathetic and noncommittal to even care. At the back of your mind you know you have everything you need to cast charm spells on all the beauties in the room like the Magician you are, but for some reason you can't manifest it tonight.

# The
# MYSTICAL PAIRING

*A true magician is creative and confident, but most of all they can exhibit power and transformation from seemingly not much at all, or from things that appear to have very little in common. It takes talent and mastery to become a magician or mixologist.*

*Whether in a forest of pines or a tequila distillery in Mexico, whether you're standing in your kitchen or in a private sacred space, follow this recipe as you would a powerful spell. Combine the tequila, lemon juice, and syrup and shake it until they become one new unique entity. Once poured into the glass, layer the Cabernet on top; let it float like a hero's cape. Last but not least, what would this drink be without a little fire? Let the flame conjure the oils of the zest, allowing it to spark and come to life.*

*If you dare drink this beverage, be prepared to let it transform you.*

Serve in　　　a rocks glass

# The
# MAGICIAN COCKTAIL

2 OUNCES AÑEJO TEQUILA

1 OUNCE LEMON JUICE

1/2 OUNCE MAPLE SYRUP

1 OUNCE CABERNET SAUVIGNON

ORANGE PEEL, FOR GARNISH [FLAME OPTIONAL]

✦

*Put the tequila, lemon juice, and maple syrup into a shaker, shake it up, and pour it over ice in a rocks glass. Float the Cabernet Sauvignon on the top and flame the orange peel.*

## Note: HOW TO FLAME AN ORANGE PEEL

*Using a citrus peeler or sharp knife, remove the skin of an orange. Be careful to avoid as much pith (white) as possible. Light a match and hold it next to the orange peel for 2 seconds. Once the water has evaporated out of the peel, squeeze and the oils of the orange will spray over the cocktail.*

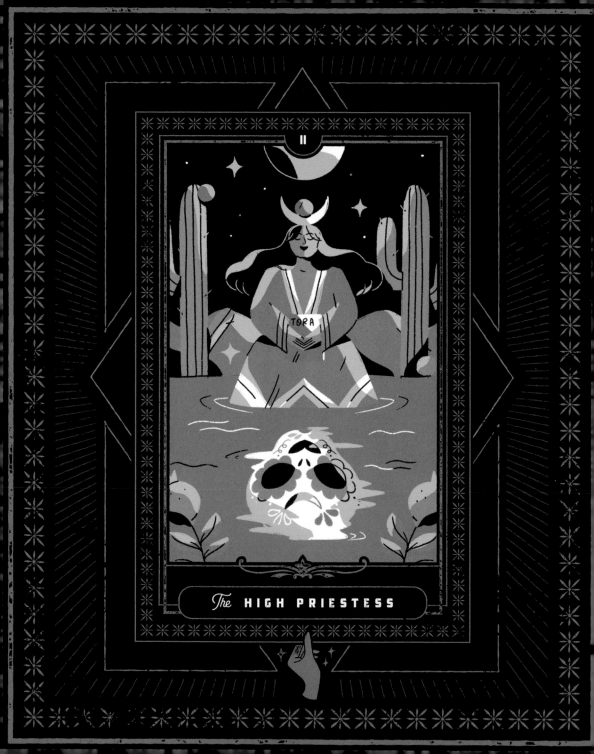

# 2 *The* HIGH PRIESTESS

✳✳✳✳✳✳✳✳✳✳✳✳✳✳✳✳✳✳✳✳✳✳✳✳✳✳✳✳✳✳✳✳✳✳✳✳

## BASIC DEFINITION

The High Priestess whispers about all things private and personal. She would love us all to look inward and find that deep quiet and knowing we have if we just listened to our intuitions. Through quieting the mind we can uncover powerful insights and truths about ourselves. Truths that can lead to our serenity and spiritual development.

## *Reversed* BASIC DEFINITION

When this deep and mysterious woman is upside-down she asks, Why don't you trust your intuition? Have you become too reliant on someone else to always call the shots for you? Have you become untrusting of your lack of spiritual connection? Do you feel that you can't or won't allow yourself to see the real truths of the universe? Or have you become fearful of the unknown?

## TEQUILA DEFINITION

Why, oh why, do we like the places we go? There's something about a particular bar or bartender that makes us feel right at home. It's just like figuring out what your favorite drink is. Maybe you can't explain it, but you know instantly this is where you want to be. Have you ever sat down with a tequila neat and contemplated your higher self? Sip and think, meditate and dream, all from the powerful sense of taste. I'm not saying that drinking will lead to higher spiritual knowing and understanding, but you never know . . .

## *Reversed* TEQUILA DEFINITION

Don't let your friends drag you to places you don't want to go, and most especially, don't let them talk you into ordering what they want you to drink or, even worse, how many drinks to have. If you aren't feeling the connection to that person your friend hooked you up with, speak the truth. If you'd rather stay in tonight and meditate rather than go out dancing, then stay in and meditate! The social butterfly in you may need a night of personal exploration; find out!

# The
# MYSTICAL PAIRING

*Underneath the light of a thin crescent moon, a bench rests atop a mossy patch that sits adjacent to your magical garden. Sleep has not come easy this night, so after making a drink, you make your way over to your spot of seclusion, barefoot and focused. You're so close to a breakthrough you can taste it. Your dreams have been so vivid that even calling them dreams is not doing them justice. These unknown visions are forcing an awakening.*

*You need a project, a momentary sidetrack. You gently tear off some of the celery leaves growing nearby and begin to carefully rip them into strips, then place them into your elixir of tequila, lemon juice, thyme, and seltzer. You raise the freshly scented glass to your nose and catch a glimpse of what was behind your eyelids. You start deciphering memories flooding back to your brain in flashes, revealing hidden truths one at a time. Following your inner guide, you take another sip, thus placing another piece in the puzzle.*

*Serve in* a collins glass

# *The*
# HIGH PRIESTESS COCKTAIL

1 OUNCE SILVER TEQUILA

1 OUNCE LEMON JUICE

1/2 OUNCE THYME AGAVE SYRUP [RECIPE FOLLOWS]

3 OUNCES CLUB SODA

THYME SPRIG AND 1 CELERY LEAF [MINCED OR TORN], FOR GARNISH

✦

*Fill a shaker with ice. Add all ingredients, except the club soda, and vigorously shake. Pour contents into a collins glass and add the club soda. Garnish with the thyme sprig and a celery leaf.*

### THYME AGAVE SYRUP

*Put 1 ounce agave, 1 ounce water, and 2 sprigs of thyme in a saucepan. Cook over medium heat, stirring, until reduced. Chill overnight and keep in the refrigerator for up to two weeks.*

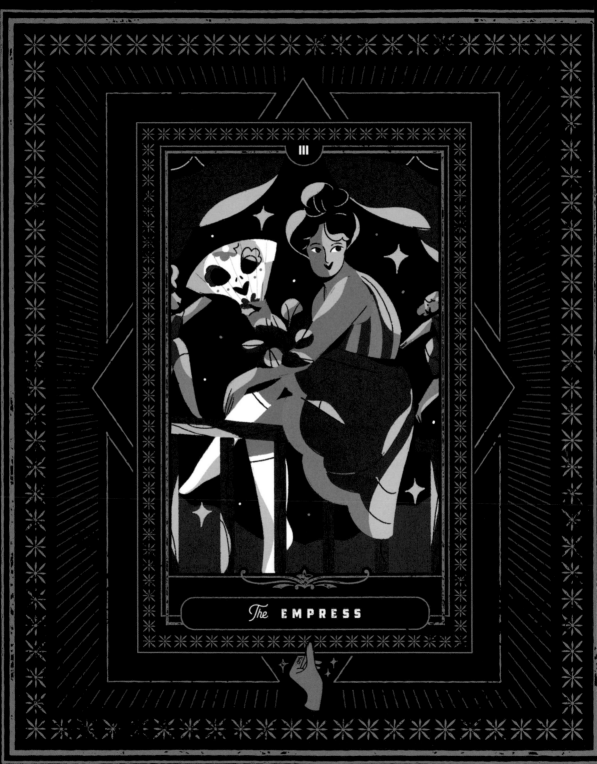

**3**       *The* **EMPRESS**

✳✳✳✳✳✳✳✳✳✳✳✳✳✳✳✳✳✳✳✳✳✳✳✳✳✳✳✳✳✳✳✳✳✳✳

## BASIC DEFINITION

The Empress teaches us to connect with beauty, love, and all things luxurious. Now is the time to create something beautiful! Go enjoy yourself and connect with your feminine energy. It speaks of your relationship with your mother and how you see yourself as a mother or nurturer, too. Maybe your maternal instinct and guidance is being called upon? Maybe you are looking to make your family a little larger . . .

## TEQUILA DEFINITION

I think it's time you went on a little vacation. Maybe one of those resort spas where you can get a massage or a facial. Afterward, when you're nice and relaxed, bundled in a comfy bathrobe and relaxing in front of a fire, breathe it in and sip on a tequila. Some bonding time with your mother or your daughter would make this experience even more rewarding. A relaxing environment makes for easier conversations where nothing is forced.

## *Reversed* BASIC DEFINITION

When this beautiful card is upside down, there is a feeling of being overly emotional. Instead of taking care of other people, you should be taking care of yourself. You've become unbalanced and are out of sync with nature and your environment. You can feel the anxiety that accompanies this lack of harmony. This card reversed can refer to infertility and uncertainty regarding your having children. You have possibly become too attached to materialism and may soon realize that happiness does not come from acquiring more things, but from within.

## *Reversed* TEQUILA DEFINITION

Don't become so overwhelmed by your creations that you start to become overly dependent. Be careful not to chase your muse down alleyways and corridors, ultimately leading to emotional disharmony and potential pain. We suffer for our art! We drink to celebrate our creations! Don't let it get to the point where your celebrating turns into dependence, negligence, and infidelity.

# The
# MYSTICAL PAIRING

*When you want to feel beautiful and loved, go for the Empress and drink it down hard. Why not treat yourself like a goddess? A ritualistic design of sensuality in abundance, this drink should be made with friends and/or lovers. Share a carafe with those who deserve, love, and nurture you.*

*The harvest of fruits with all of its tastes and smells—as if wine wasn't delicious enough on its own, think of adding nectar, lime, and a hint of basil. When imbibing a couple of these drinks, you can be sure others will taste and feel the power of a strong, bold woman!*

*Serve in*  *a wineglass*

# *The*
# EMPRESS COCKTAIL

1/2 OUNCE REPOSADO TEQUILA

1 OUNCE MANGO NECTAR

1/2 OUNCE FRESH LIME JUICE

4 OUNCES SPARKLING WINE

FRESH BASIL LEAF

✦

*Fill a shaker with ice and add the tequila, mango nectar, and lime juice. Shake well and pour into a traditional wineglass. Top with the sparkling wine. Garnish with a spanked basil leaf—simply clap the basil leaf between your hands to bring out the aromatics.*

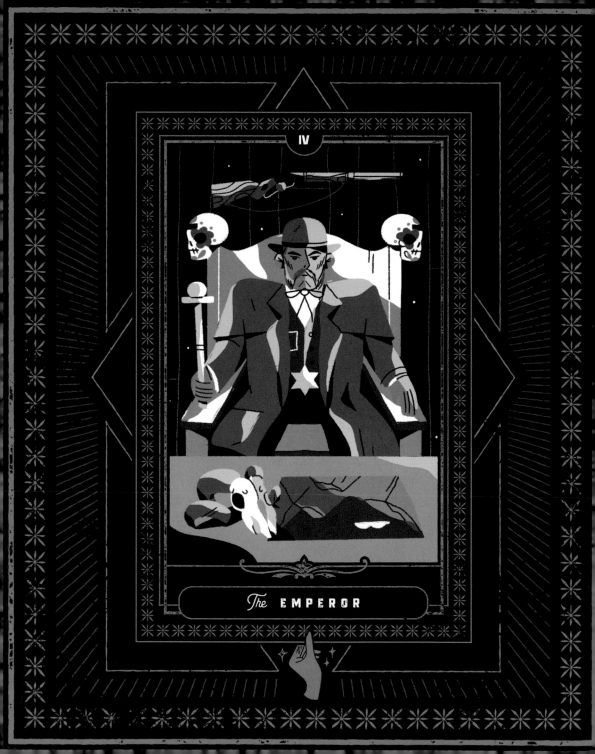

The EMPEROR

# *The* EMPEROR

✳✳✳✳✳✳✳✳✳✳✳✳✳✳✳✳✳✳✳✳✳✳✳✳✳✳✳✳✳✳✳✳

## BASIC DEFINITION

The Emperor reminds us that we can all use some control and structure to keep us safe and out of the way of chaos. Can you hear your father's voice in your head? Reminding you to always make smart choices. Reinforcing the importance of taking action and thinking things through. Always remembering to dot your I's and cross your T's and to please make sure to submit your taxes on time. Your father is only looking out for you, and so is the Emperor.

## TEQUILA DEFINITION

Sometimes we'd love to eyeball a drink recipe and hope we are close to the actual measurements, but that one friend you know won't let that happen. They're always going by the recipe book, systematically following the order of ingredients by how they're listed and measuring out exactly the right amount for everyone. They're the person planning your night to the smallest detail and making sure everyone is safe, and the designated driver remains sober. The Emperor might not be the most fun at parties, but they're very necessary. Just imagine if we didn't have anyone checking on us or having our backs if a fight broke out.

## *Reversed* BASIC DEFINITION

Your father is there to protect you and offer his controlled guidance, but what happens if his advice isn't advice at all, but rather a dominant misuse of power? He is so headstrong that his leadership becomes tyrannical. He's not really guiding you to make the right choices but dominating you into making the choices he wants you to make.

## *Reversed* TEQUILA DEFINITION

You know that person who always has to be in control all of the time? When you're out gallivanting about town, no one needs the stubborn or inflexible friend keeping you from having fun and, dare I say, getting a little out of control. There is a time and place for everything. And right now, the time and place is screaming to relax and let go of the busy, work-filled day that just ended.

# The
# MYSTICAL PAIRING

*Embodying the Emperor is embracing your masculine energy. Whenever you need to channel traits and attributes such as leadership, maturity, and discipline, why not start with a ritual that will solidify it and make it realized?*

*Gather your ingredients and don't substitute anything! Structure and rule following are part of this ritual. Everything is needed, from the tart cranberry flavor of the hibiscus to the bold heat of the habanero. This powerful drink should be made when you need a boost of confidence! Maybe you're a leader but you're not feeling much like one? This potion can help do the trick.*

*When you're feeling comfortable in your home bar, start whispering the words of confidence you need to hear. As you're shaking the first of the ingredients, continue these words of reassurance. As the cocktail starts coming together, let your words become louder. And after you take your first sip, feel the magical control enter your being and become the person you need to be!*

*Serve in* *a double rocks glass*

# *The*
# EMPEROR COCKTAIL

1 1/2 OUNCES REPOSADO TEQUILA

1/2 OUNCE MEZCAL

3 OUNCES ORANGE JUICE

1 OUNCE HIBISCUS HABANERO SYRUP [RECIPE FOLLOWS]

1/2 OUNCE 151 RUM

DEHYDRATED ORANGE, FOR GARNISH

✦

*Put the tequila, mezcal, and orange juice in a shaker.*
*Pour the hibiscus habanero syrup into the bottom of*
*a double rocks glass with ice. Slowly add the shaker*
*mixture on top to avoid integrating. Float the rum on*
*top. Garnish with the dehydrated orange.*

### HIBISCUS HABANERO SYRUP

*Put 1 cup superfine sugar, 1 cup water, and two habaneros in a small*
*saucepan. Bring to a boil and then add 1 hibiscus tea bag and steep for about*
*5 minutes. Stir until the sugar dissolves. Discard the habaneros after an hour.*
*Chill overnight and keep in the refrigerator for up to two weeks.*

THE HIEROPHANT

# 5 · *The* HIEROPHANT

## BASIC DEFINITION

There's something to be said about the systems that work well in your life. Why would you ever want to stray from a solid, proven, conventional tradition? Have you ever thought about joining a large organization or church because there is a security and assurance that comes along with it? It's good to have a priest or spiritual advisor to rely upon in times of inner crisis. It can provide a peace in knowing that there is a divine power out there, and we need to have faith that it knows the right way to go.

## *Reversed* BASIC DEFINITION

Nothing says you have to follow the rigid guidelines of traditional religion or popular consensus. The Hierophant Reversed says it's okay to rebel against popular beliefs and social norms. Maybe the current systems are becoming outdated and abused? Maybe you can see through the hypocrisy and abuse of power to the point where you are now on your own path? Stagnation and confinement have become dirty words.

## TEQUILA DEFINITION

If your favorite drink from your most treasured bar is gaining popularity, you can take solace in knowing that your taste is shared by many. You may be content in knowing that your place of power is now becoming busier and more successful. It's also possible that your veteran status as a regular at this watering hole has placed you in a position of trusted advisor or guru.

## *Reversed* TEQUILA DEFINITIONS

The wedding is three weeks away and it is looking to be a huge event. Nerves have you and your fiancé opening a bottle of tequila and toasting to the large event when you both stop, glasses frozen, eyes locked, and at the same time say, "Screw this! Let's elope." Why do what everyone expects of you? You were both coerced into this expensive wedding, and no one bothered to ask what you really wanted, which was VEGAS, BABY!

# *The* MYSTICAL PAIRING

*Cheers to tradition! Whether you're toasting before Christmas dinner or as an accompaniment to candle-light on Midwinter's Eve, this recipe will mark a place in your life as deep as tattooed ink.*

*Gather around your friends and sisters. This is a time of love and light. Before you take up the drink to commemorate this festive event, form your circle and hold your hands. Offer a wish and a blessing for one another, then get to work on those potions! Smell the elderberry and sage. Taste the cherries and let them carry you away to when you were small and tradition, like family, is what kept you safe and loved.*

*Serve in*    *a double rocks glass*

# The
# HIEROPHANT COCKTAIL

2 TO 3 PITTED CHERRIES, MUDDLED, PLUS 1 FOR GARNISH

2 OUNCES HENDRICK'S GIN

1/2 OUNCE ST. GERMAIN

1 OUNCE LEMON JUICE

1/2 OUNCE SAGE SIMPLE SYRUP [RECIPE FOLLOWS]

1 FRESH SAGE SPRIG, FOR GARNISH

✦

*Place the muddled cherries into a shaker. Add the rest of the ingredients and ice, shake vigorously, and strain into a double rocks glass over more ice. Garnish with a pitted cherry and sage sprig.*

### SAGE SIMPLE SYRUP

*Put 1 cup sugar, 1 cup water, and 10 sage leaves, with or without stems, into a small saucepan. Bring to a boil and stir until the sugar has dissolved. Chill overnight and keep in the refrigerator for up to two weeks.*

# 6

# *The* **LOVERS**

✳✳✳✳✳✳✳✳✳✳✳✳✳✳✳✳✳✳✳✳✳✳✳✳✳✳✳✳✳✳✳✳✳✳✳✳✳✳

## BASIC DEFINITION

If you're looking for love, then this is the card you want to see. Not only does it mean the relationship you are entering into is a good one, but also that you both are equally aligned and will make good important choices together. It can signify a powerful friendship, as well. The Lovers reminds us that we have to allow ourselves to be ready for inevitable change that comes with giving up a part of ourselves to another. Be ready: It's a higher love!

## TEQUILA DEFINITION

How can you stay at home when the woman of your dreams is pouring drinks at your favorite bar? You know that one day you'll have the courage to take this casual relationship to the next level and ask her on a date. You hope the free drinks and sly smile are just for you. How can you know for sure? The Lovers asks you to trust in your heart; if it's meant to be, then it's meant to be.

## *Reversed* BASIC DEFINITION

The Lovers Reversed refers to bad choices in—but not exclusive to—bad relationships. When the Lovers Reversed shows up in a reading it can sometimes mean divorce or separation. Or losing faith in yourself and a lack of self-love could explain why you are making bad relationship choices and decisions. Words like "codependency" and "manipulation" may ring some bells when you see the Lovers Reversed. There may be too many differences to continue on with your current partner, as well.

## *Reversed* TEQUILA DEFINITION

Let's talk about bad choices. You know that friend or lover who is always pulling you into their drama and bad decisions? The friend that leaves you at the bar to find your own way home after they have found someone to hook up with. The Lover who drinks too much and starts a fight with you on a regular basis. The one who, when inebriated, constantly makes poor choices and threatens separation. Maybe it's time you find your own ride home or someone who doesn't have so many issues.

# *The* MYSTICAL PAIRING

*Who doesn't love to be in love? Whether you are looking to strengthen the connection with your lover or embark on a passage of self-love, this is the ritual for you.*

*Let's start with tying a simple red string to your and your lover's wrists as a symbol of your connection. Leaving enough slack to make the drinks together, and at the same time. Start with a kind declaration to each other. This drink recipe is a ritual of labor and love in and of itself. The act of manifesting the drinks together will only make your relationship stronger! When consuming the intoxicating and romantic flavors, remember when you two first met and understand why you make the right combination.*

*And if you are drinking these alone? Place the glasses side by side, a straw gently resting in each glass and, together all at once, drink to self-love and the possibility of a new love to come.*

*Serve in* a rocks glass

# *The*
# LOVERS COCKTAILS
# LOVER #1

---

1 OUNCE NAVY-STRENGTH RUM

1 OUNCE BLACK RUM

2 OUNCES ORANGE JUICE

1 OUNCE COCONUT CREAM

3/4 OUNCE LIME JUICE

1 OUNCE CINNAMON BARK SYRUP [RECIPE FOLLOWS]

1 TABLESPOON ACTIVATED CHARCOAL

2 STRAWBERRY SLICES, FOR GARNISH

✦

*Add all the ingredients into a blender with ice and blend. Garnish with the strawberry slices.*

### CINNAMON BARK SYRUP

*Muddle 1 cinnamon stick into shards and transfer to a small saucepan with 1 cup water and 1 cup sugar. Slowly bring the mixture to almost a boil, reduce the heat, and simmer for 4 minutes. Chill overnight and keep in the refrigerator for up to two weeks.*

# *The*
# LOVERS COCKTAILS
# LOVER #2

---

1 OUNCE BARBADOS RUM

1 OUNCE LIGHT RUM

2 OUNCES ORANGE JUICE

1 OUNCE STRAWBERRY PUREE

3/4 OUNCE LIME JUICE

1 OUNCE SIMPLE SYRUP [RECIPE FOLLOWS]

2 STRAWBERRY SLICES, FOR GARNISH

✦

*Add all of the ingredients into a blender with ice and blend. Garnish with the strawberry slices.*

### SIMPLE SYRUP

*In a saucepan, combine 1 cup water with 1 cup sugar and bring to a boil. Wait until all the sugar is dissolved. Chill overnight and keep in the refrigerator for up to two weeks.*

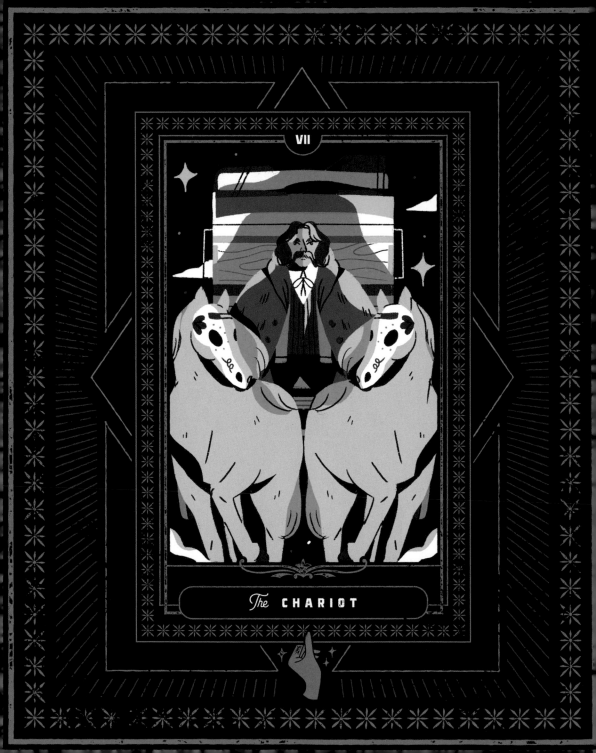

# 7

# *The* CHARIOT

## BASIC DEFINITION

When the Chariot shows up in a reading, it's a very good sign. Whether it's regarding work, travel, decisions, or relationships, it speaks to victory, success, action, and confidence! Everything you need to make sure you triumph over the obstacles laid out before you. The Chariot's prosperity comes from your own willpower and drive. You want it bad enough, you will make it happen.

## *Reversed* BASIC DEFINITION

When the Chariot is upside down, instead of knowing exactly what you want and having the desire and willpower to go out and get it, you are apathetic and misdirected. Your self-discipline may be slipping away, and you feel like you are going in the wrong direction or stuck in a circle or holding pattern. You need to make sure you recover your inner purpose and focus. Just like the imagery on the tarot card, if the creatures pulling your cart are going in opposite directions, you will remain stationary.

## TEQUILA DEFINITION

It's good to be in control of a situation. Wherever you are headed on this magically filled night you will be blessed with success. Why? Because you are the type of person that can make things happen. Your favorite restaurant has no available tables, but somehow you know the owner and you get seated. You take your lover dancing, and nothing will get in your way from having an amazing Chariot-filled, date-night experience.

## *Reversed* TEQUILA DEFINITION

You had such high hopes as your night got underway. You made all the arrangements, picked up your friends, and started on your way to the new tequila bar you heard such great things about. Unfortunately, on your way there, construction and a series of other unfortunate events prevented you from arriving at your destination even remotely close to when you wanted. Now you are frustrated and your friends are getting impatient. After another twenty minutes of traffic, you start questioning whether you still even want to go to the stupid tequila bar. I guess it's up to you to see if you can salvage the Chariot in reverse.

# *The* MYSTICAL PAIRING

*Anyone can make a traditional Moscow Mule, but it takes someone with focus, drive, and a progressive mind to make the Chariot.*

*Instead of vodka, let tequila pull you along with this beverage. Why stop at lime when you can add the bold flavors of apples and beets? Be ambitious! Make this cocktail when you need to jump-start your life in the right direction. When profit is knocking at your door and you're reaching out to open it, bring this drink to your lips. Let the cocktail push you onward: Let it focus your energy forward and go along for the ride. Don't be afraid of all that momentum—just make sure to hold on, because it'll only bring you victory!*

*Serve in*     *a collins glass*

# *The* CHARIOT COCKTAIL

1 1/2 OUNCES BLANCO TEQUILA

3/4 OUNCE BEET JUICE

1/2 OUNCE LIME JUICE

1 OUNCE UNFILTERED APPLE CIDER

A SPLASH OF GINGER BEER

1 LIME SLICE, FOR GARNISH

✦

*Place the tequila, beet and lime juices, and apple cider into a shaker. Shake well and strain into a collins glass filled with ice. Top with the ginger beer and garnish with a slice of lime.*

# 8

# STRENGTH

## BASIC DEFINITION

It's easy to think of physical strength when you see this card, but the Strength card most often refers to inner strength. Do you have the self-discipline and the peaceful yet powerful resolve to be an influencer to get what you want? Can you open the jaws of the lion's mouth and bring your head closely inside where it now becomes a matter of trust and mutual respect? Strength can also refer to being in good health and having enough energy in reserve so you don't become so exhausted.

## *Reversed* BASIC DEFINITION

Strength in reverse often refers to doubting yourself, your fear of control or of being a good leader. Everyone at some time in their lives experiences apprehension and the feeling of being small. We think cowardly thoughts and worry if we will ever be strong enough to live the way we want to live. Stop doubting yourself! You are not a fragile little thing. The only thing blocking you from being your best self is you.

## TEQUILA DEFINITION

Have you ever been on a bar crawl? Have you learned the trick to survival? You can't start off too strong, right? It's a marathon and not a sprint, as they say. You need to conserve your strength. Utilize your self-discipline and endurance so you can continue on long after your friends. You'll still be going strong while they'll be on the floor, due to not paying attention to their own tolerance or lack thereof.

## *Reversed* TEQUILA DEFINITION

Have you ever been invited to a college party or social gathering where you didn't know many people and were trying to make a good first impression by being the life of the party? Has someone ever tested your strength and willpower by seeing how "cool" you were by how much you could drink? I know you wanted to impress everyone, but you can't allow yourself to become peer-pressured into a losing situation. Were you strong enough to say "no"? Are you still strong enough to say no when you don't want to partake in a night of careless drinking? Don't give in! Stand your ground, and people will respect you even more.

# _The_ MYSTICAL PAIRING

Sometimes people drink to escape. Other times we drink to embrace. When the time comes to connect with our inner discipline and tranquility, reach for the right ingredients and begin this strong ritual of change.

After a particularly long day at work, one where your voice was stifled and your actions were questioned, grab your glass and head outside. Maybe after a gentle rain, when the grass glistens off the moonlight, stand on your porch and say the words out loud you wished you said earlier.

Let the turmeric and lemon revitalize you—smell the zest in the air! Scream a lion's roar into the night and say, "I am strong!" three times, each time louder than the one before until you believe it. Each time filled with so much strength and passion, everyone who can hear you believes it, too. "I am strong!"

_Serve in_     _a rocks glass_

# *The* STRENGTH COCKTAIL

---

**2 OUNCES OLD TOM GIN**

**1/2 OUNCE TURMERIC HONEY SYRUP [RECIPE FOLLOWS]**

**1 OUNCE FRESH LEMON JUICE**

**BLACK SEA SALT, FOR GARNISH**

**LEMON PEEL, FOR GARNISH**

✦

*Place the gin, syrup, and lemon juice into a shaker. Shake vigorously and strain over ice into a rocks glass. Garnish with the black sea salt. Twist the lemon peel over the cocktail to release its oils.*

### TURMERIC HONEY SYRUP

*In a small saucepan, bring 1 cup of honey, 1 cup of water, 1 teaspoon turmeric, and 10 black peppercorns to a boil. Gently stir until the honey is dissolved. Chill overnight and keep in the refrigerator for up to two weeks.*

# 9

*The* **HERMIT**

## BASIC DEFINITION

The Hermit whispers that now is the perfect time for inner reflection and quiet solitude. Life is a journey and during that voyage you may want or need time to reflect on how far you've come, both physically or spiritually. Either way, the Hermit is a time of soul searching. Life can pile up sometimes and even become a bit of a mess. When this happens, it's always a good idea to find your inner voice and let that feeling guide you to a quiet, more peaceful place.

## TEQUILA DEFINITION

Too much partying has left you feeling vacant and abused. You are journeying further and further away from your true north. Staying up later than usual is affecting your internal clock, and you aren't listening to the needs of your body. The next couple of weekends you start declining invitations from friends so you can start your personal journey of reassessment, truth, and illumination.

## *Reversed* BASIC DEFINITION

There will also be times in your spiritual journey where you may find that you have hit a bump in the road and have undertaken a personal setback. You aren't interested in listening to your friends and family try to help you. You may be going through an immature phase and feeling a powerful disconnection with society. You start isolating yourself for the wrong reasons. You may think that you need to be alone but what you actually need is to heal—and you can't do that by isolating yourself.

## *Reversed* TEQUILA DEFINITION

Do you have that friend or family member who vanishes? One day, out of the blue, they just disappear? Life becomes too difficult and they choose to take a little trip that turns out to be a destructive, lonely bender. Some people make hasty decisions that lead down roads to other continuous bad decisions. It may sound a bit like a romance novel, but there's nothing romantic about winding up in a dive bar in Key West, passed out and alone. Rejoin society!

# The
# MYSTICAL PAIRING

*Drinking alone is most often associated with negative connotations. But what if you were drinking in solitude to do a little soul searching? Being alone with your thoughts can bring self-awareness. Withdrawing from society every now and again can actually bring you closer to enlightenment if you let it.*

*Maybe take the weekend and do a little fishing. Head to that cabin in the wilderness, the one you've been going to since you were a child. Bring some music, your tackle box, and a journal to write down your self-discovery.*

*Before going to bed that first night, prepare this cocktail on the porch overlooking the lake and underneath the stars. As you're mixing the ingredients, breathe in the unique smells. The caraway, anise, and Chartreuse make for an intoxicating aroma. If you have the willpower to appreciate this drink before imbibing, then you've already begun your journey. Embrace it!*

*Serve in*     *a collins glass*

# The
# HERMIT COCKTAIL

1 1/2 OUNCES AQUAVIT

3/4 OUNCE LEMON JUICE

1/2 OUNCE YELLOW CHARTREUSE

1/2 OUNCE HONEY SIMPLE SYRUP [RECIPE FOLLOWS]

1 BARSPOON GREEK YOGURT

SPLASH OF CLUB SODA

1 LEMON WEDGE, FOR GARNISH

✦

*Add the aquavit, lemon juice, Chartreuse, honey simple syrup, and yogurt to a shaker. Mix and pour into a collins glass with nugget ice (see below). Top with club soda and garnish with the lemon wedge.*

### HONEY SIMPLE SYRUP

*Put 1 cup honey and 1 cup water into a saucepan and cook over medium heat until the mixture has reduced somewhat and come together. Let chill overnight and keep in the refrigerator for up to two weeks.*

### Note: NUGGET ICE

*Nugget ice is made from flaked ice and looks like small pebbles. They have a lot of air in them and are very chewable. Crushed ice would do the trick, too.*

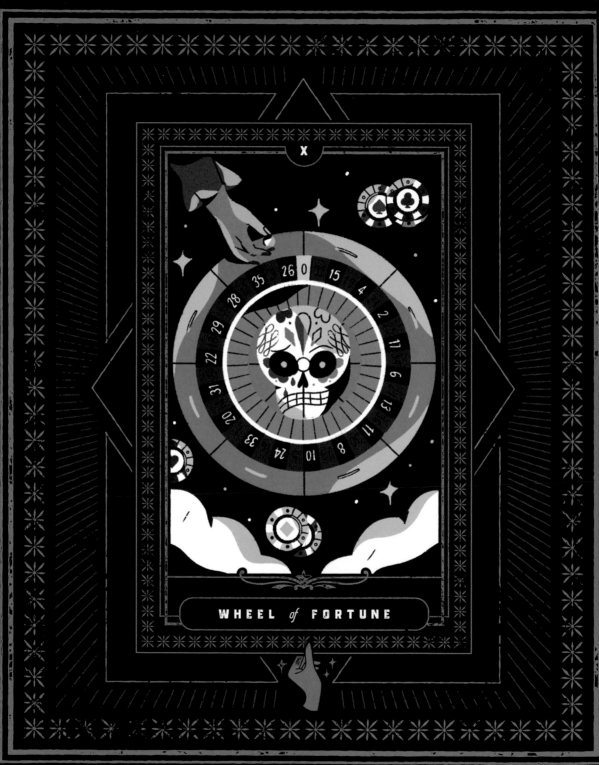

# 10 The WHEEL of FORTUNE

✳✳✳✳✳✳✳✳✳✳✳✳✳✳✳✳✳✳✳✳✳✳✳✳✳✳✳✳✳✳✳✳✳✳✳✳

## BASIC DEFINITION

When the Wheel of Fortune shows up in a reading, you have come to a positive turning point in your life. This is exciting stuff! Life changes every three months from good to bad and back to good again. The cycle of life is constantly turning. And a lot of that is completely out of our control. With this tarot card, an unexpected change of good fortune has entered your life and you can feel it. Maybe a resolution around a concern you've been worrying about has just turned out very positive. Maybe you'll receive a windfall of cash. Whatever it is, look forward to some good fortune. You deserve it!

## Reversed BASIC DEFINITION

Just like there will be periods of good luck coming your way, the wheel also turns upside down and with that so does your luck. The Wheel Reversed reminds us that we are all the same. We are all both lucky and unlucky. We shouldn't take things personally when we are facing one of the downturns of life. We just have to ride it out. The best we can ask for is that we learn valuable lessons when the reversed Wheel comes rolling in. Instead of fighting the negativity, try relinquishing control and just accept this as an unexpected setback. In a few months the reversed Wheel will turn right side up again and you will have yet another reversal of fortune.

## TEQUILA DEFINITION

Take a trip to Las Vegas when this card turns up in a reading. What could possibly go wrong when you combine mucho tequila and gambling? Normally, I'd recommend staying away from this type of situation, but if you're feeling lucky, maybe the success of the Wheel of Fortune will keep turning in your favor. Maybe a casino will comp your room when they see your winning streak. Or, at the very least, they won't charge you for all those tequilas you've been drinking.

## Reversed TEQUILA DEFINITION

Before you lose any more money or make any more bad decisions, just stop what you are doing and immediately go home. This isn't your night. Some things are out of your control, and this night has gotten away from you. Tequila is usually your friend, but not tonight. Whether it was one too many or you were on a mission of self-destruction, you need to retreat to fight another day. Your friends still love you, even though you might have been an embarrassing mess. This bad luck will turn good again, as the Wheel is always turning.

# The
# MYSTICAL PAIRING

*The Wheel of Fortune's very nature is one of luck and chance. Make this cocktail when you need to change your energy from bad to good. It's one thing to say you're going to be more positive and give off joyful energy but ritualizing the change of perception will make it more grounded in reality.*

*Before the cocktail preparation begins, create a sacred space, one that is free of clutter, and the feng shui of the room will work to your benefit. When feeling comfortable, burn some dried sage in a counterclockwise motion and say, "Thank you for removing any negative energy, and I welcome any and all positivity and light into my life."*

*Once the pregame is completed, start making that cocktail! With tastes and smells of jasmine, honey, and mint, how can there possibly be any negative energy remaining?*

*Serve in*     *a collins glass*

# *The*
# WHEEL OF FORTUNE COCKTAIL

### 1 1/2 OUNCES NOLET'S GIN

### 4 OUNCES JASMINE MATCHA ICED GREEN TEA [RECIPE FOLLOWS]

### 1/2 OUNCE YUZU HONEY SYRUP [RECIPE FOLLOWS]

### 6 FRESH MINT LEAVES, PLUS 1 SPRIG, FOR GARNISH

✦

*Put all of the ingredients into a shaker with ice and shake well (this allows the mint to accent the tea). Serve in a collins glass with ice. Garnish with a mint sprig.*

#### JASMINE MATCHA ICED GREEN TEA

*Put 6 cups of water and two tea bags into a saucepan. Cook over medium heat until boiling, then steep for 10 minutes. Let chill overnight and keep in the refrigerator for up to two weeks.*

#### YUZU HONEY SYRUP

*Put 1/4 ounce yuzu extract, 1 cup honey, and 1 cup water into a saucepan and cook over medium heat until the mixture is reduced. Let chill overnight and keep in the refrigerator for up to two weeks.*

# JUSTICE

✳✳✳✳✳✳✳✳✳✳✳✳✳✳✳✳✳✳✳✳✳✳✳✳✳✳✳✳✳✳✳✳

## BASIC DEFINITION

When Justice appears in your reading, have the security in knowing that law, balance, and fairness will be on your side. If you are facing a legal matter, know that things will work out the way you would like them to. Also, realize that you may be called accountable for a past action. But don't worry: If you treated others fairly in the past, then I'm sure you will be treated fairly now. Karma, karma, karma! Keep a level head when you see Justice in your reading, and make sure you have your priorities in order.

## *Reversed* BASIC DEFINITION

If Justice keeps things fair, then Justice Reversed teaches us that life is at times unfair, too. Not everyone you meet will be as objective and accountable as you. Some people are dishonest, corrupt, and even biased about their decisions and choices. Any legal matters you're involved in at the moment will unfortunately not turn out the way you would like. I hope it isn't because you mistreated others in the past and this is karma's way of getting its revenge. Justice Reversed will punish those who think they are above the law.

## TEQUILA DEFINITION

Isn't it a great feeling when you buy a friend a drink and they offer to pick up the next round? Good friends like to keep things fair. It shouldn't even be discussed ahead of time. Any good bar behavior depends on truth, balance, and fairness. Be responsible for your choices and always keep perspective. If someone doesn't offer to repay your good deed, know that the universe will find a way to adjust itself to make things right. Buy that beauty sitting next to you a drink without any further motive other than paying it forward. See where that gets you!

## *Reversed* TEQUILA DEFINITION

It wasn't your intention to get behind the wheel of your SUV after drinking all that tequila. You thought, because it was only a few miles away, you could easily make it home without anything going wrong. It's never a good idea to get behind the wheel when intoxicated. Remembering you pulled the reversed Justice card that morning, maybe you should have chosen to be the designated driver. The police officer pulling you over because you failed to make a turn signal doesn't care that you had the best of intentions in mind or that you live just a mile farther down the road. Karma is indeed a bitch!

# *The* MYSTICAL PAIRING

*I wish for all of your interactions with others to be balanced and fair. It's a wonderful thought, but I know it's not a realistic one. When the time beckons for fairness and justice to prevail, consider this cocktail to balance those emotions that may be spinning a bit out of control.*

*This cocktail is a Jenga game: the definition of balance. The citrus from the Aperol and the pineapple-infused tequila resonate perfectly with the three types of bitters used. The use of the bitters and Chartreuse continue to balance out the cocktail while making it more complex.*

*When preparing this cocktail sit in front of a mirror if you can. Watch yourself make the drink as if you're looking at yourself through someone else's eyes. Look upon yourself as you would have others look upon you. Say the words "I am just and I am fair, I give it out and will get it back" eleven times once the cocktail is ready to be consumed. Then enjoy the Justice!*

*Serve in* — *a rocks glass*

# *The*
# JUSTICE COCKTAIL

1 OUNCE PINEAPPLE-INFUSED TEQUILA

1 OUNCE APEROL

1 OUNCE YELLOW CHARTREUSE

1 DASH ORANGE BITTERS

1 DASH GRAPEFRUIT BITTERS

1 DASH SCRAPPY'S FIREWATER HABANERO TINCTURE BITTERS

1 GRAPEFRUIT WEDGE, FOR GARNISH

✦

*Stir together all the ingredients in a mixing glass with
ice and strain over 1 large ice cube. Garnish with the
grapefruit wedge.*

# 12 *The* HANGED MAN

## BASIC DEFINITION

The Hanged Man says you need to change your perspective and outlook in order to grow. By truly letting go of your old way of thinking you can achieve a newfound wisdom. You may need to sacrifice a part of yourself to achieve this new level of enlightenment, but it'll all be worth it. Take an intentional pause. Just like the man on the card, whose face is at peace. He put himself in this position in order to see the world differently. It's a trial of sorts. The things we will do for spiritual growth . . .

## TEQUILA DEFINITION

Another night watching life pass you by. What's got you so down? You're out and about, on the town, tequila in hand, but you're not smiling. What's wrong? This is your idea of fun, isn't it? Maybe you're getting a bit bored of this routine so the following weekend you make a conscious decision to stay home. You pour yourself a drink and watch a movie. It may be boring and you might miss being social but you're smiling, because you know this is exactly what you needed.

## *Reversed* BASIC DEFINITION

You should never have to sacrifice yourself for little or no change. When you are making yourself uncomfortable on purpose you should at least be getting something out of it in return, right? The Hanged Man Reversed tells you that your inability to change is really holding you back. Valuing the material over the spiritual isn't serving you right now. Why are you avoiding any chance of real growth or change? Perhaps you are content with the way life is going at the moment but, if that was the case, why are you hanging upside down?

## *Reversed* TEQUILA DEFINITION

Separating yourself from a group of friends who are partying way more than they should is not an easy thing to do. You've invested so much time with these people only to realize that their behavior has become destructive. It's not an easy choice, but you can't hold on to things that aren't working for you. You're going to have to just rip off the Band-Aid and say goodbye.

# *The* MYSTICAL PAIRING

*How far would you go to try something new? How far would you fare out of your comfort zone? Would you sacrifice consistency for a taste of the unknown? Sometimes life calls you to renounce the old ways and embrace the new. Such an offering may also look like a trial one needs to endure with patience. Attempt this ritual and change your perspective!*

*You and two friends (a group of three) under a desert moon, embrace this odd prickly pear fruit. How could something that looks so strange taste so good? It's both sweet and sour, yin and yang, masculine strength and feminine ways. As you sacrifice the fruit to this cocktail, say thank you to the old ways that have served you well, but look forward to the new beautiful you!*

*And dive in!*

*Serve in* a collins glass

# _The_
# HANGED MAN COCKTAIL

1 1/2 OUNCES BLANCO TEQUILA

1 1/2 OUNCES XOCONOSTLE CACTUS SYRUP [RECIPE FOLLOWS]

2 OUNCES CLUB SODA

1 PRICKLY PEAR WEDGE, FOR GARNISH

✦

_Put all of the ingredients into a shaker with ice. Shake it like you mean it. Serve in a collins glass, over ice, and garnish with the prickly pear wedge._

### XOCONOSTLE CACTUS SYRUP

_Put 1 cup water, 1 cup sugar, and juice from three xoconostle cacti into a small saucepan. Cook over medium heat until the sugar is dissolved. Let chill overnight and keep in the refrigerator for up to two weeks._

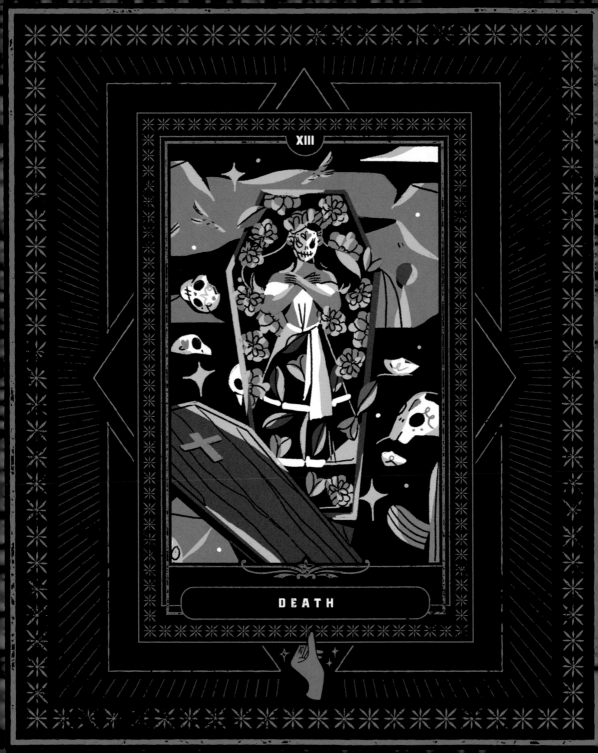

# 13

# DEATH

## BASIC DEFINITION

Death is a part of life and, as such, when the Death card comes up in a reading it can also mean rebirth. A change is happening to you and with it comes an invitation to transform into a more powerful you. Just like when a caterpillar changes into a butterfly, Death is the cocoon stage. Emerging from the cycle of transformation, you will see the world differently and ultimately have a completely new belief system. Face it, you're a new person, and there is no going back to the old you. Just like you cannot come back to life once you have died, you have to accept the end to have a new beginning.

## TEQUILA DEFINITION

How long have you been a vodka person? I get it, it's been your go-to drink for as long as you can remember, but here comes your crazy, eccentric friend pushing tequila all up in your grill. It's not a big deal, right? Trying a new drink: what could go wrong? Are you worried it'll be so transformative you'll come out of this a changed human being? Will you be able to say goodbye to the old you and embrace this new beginning of sorts? I'm not saying you will have to start talking in a southern drawl and riding horses, I'm just telling you to embrace the inevitable. Enjoy tequila!

## *Reversed* BASIC DEFINITION

With every new chapter starting in your life there has to be one that closes. How will you accept the new entry in your life? Will you suffer the loss so greatly and deeply that you will not allow yourself to enjoy the next part of your life? Death Reversed warns that your fear of the unknown will prohibit you from moving forward. And what happens when you move on? You grow and you learn and you evolve. So many things can happen. Any significant change can make you think of your own mortality. With the changing of the seasons we are reminded of death and rebirth all the time. Let go of the fear of change and live your best life!

## *Reversed* TEQUILA DEFINITION

Congratulations! You graduated college and now you have the rest of your life to look forward to. Yet leaving the college lifestyle behind and, with that, all of the great friends you've accumulated along the way, is scary. Death in reverse warns you about clinging to those last four years and denying yourself the gift of change that is knocking on your door. It's sad to think about moving back home in order to start fresh when it feels like you are somehow going backward. Do yourself a favor: After you've said goodbye to the college you, pour yourself a tequila on the rocks and toast yourself to the beginning of your adult life.

# The
# MYSTICAL PAIRING

*Let's all raise our glasses and drink to our rebirth! Whether you want to activate a transformation in your life or celebrate a significant change that has already happened, this is the drink for you. But, be warned. This drink is not for the faint of heart. Have you ever peered into the blackest of nights? Well, when you make this cocktail, you will. Before you drink this powerful concoction be sure you are prepared to accept the magic of change.*

*On any normal, ordinary evening you can initiate significant change. Share this transformation with friends who will love you for who you are and who you will become. The more friends that embrace in the magic, the greater the ritual it will become.*

*Serve in*     *a double rocks glass*

# The
# DEATH COCKTAIL

1 1/2 OUNCES BLANCO TEQUILA

1/2 OUNCE MEZCAL

2 OUNCES FRESH LIME JUICE

1 OUNCE ACTIVATED CHARCOAL SYRUP
(RECIPE FOLLOWS)

1 LIME WHEEL, FOR GARNISH

✦

*Place all ingredients into a shaker and shake vigorously. Serve this cocktail on the rocks in a double rocks glass. Garnish with a lime wheel.*

### ACTIVATED CHARCOAL SYRUP

*Put 1 cup water, 1 cup agave syrup, and 1 tablespoon activated charcoal into a saucepan and cook over medium heat for 15 minutes until the mixture dissolves and reduces, becoming uniform. Let chill overnight and keep in the refrigerator for up to two weeks.*

# 14

# TEMPERANCE

## BASIC DEFINITION

The Temperance card says it's time for patience. When you can find the time to quiet your mind and hear what's going on inside yourself, is when you can truly find balance, synergy, and restraint. When your inner voice says moderation and neutrality, please listen to it. Sometimes better things do indeed come to those who wait. The important thing is, when you are practicing harmony between all things and the "less is more" concept, are you truly being here now? Temperance is a life lesson, but you really have to listen to your angels and the messages they are sending you. How do you ask?

Through meditation and inner listening.

## *Reversed* BASIC DEFINITION

When your life feels unbalanced and your relationship with yourself or with others feels like oil and water, you may be feeling some Temperance Reversed energy. The need to go to extremes and do things excessively may lead to very bad choices—choices that you will most likely regret later on. Don't let yourself be forced into decisions you are not prepared to make because someone might be impatient or frustrated with your behavior. Temperance Reversed says you need to reevaluate how you go about doing things in your life. Maybe you just need to stop what you're doing and breathe.

Regain your inner balance.

## TEQUILA DEFINITION

What, in your opinion, makes the perfect drink? For me obviously, it has tequila in it. But, in all seriousness, the perfect drink is a balanced combination of the most ideal ingredients to create a masterpiece of alchemy. A beautiful blending of flavors to find the most delicious of tastes. It takes restraint and patience to pour the proper amount of tequila for the drink to be just right. You may want to keep pouring but you know if you overdo it, the drink will suffer. How many of my bartender friends have truly struggled through the art of creating the most flawless cocktail? Synergy is everything!

## *Reversed* TEQUILA DEFINITION

I'll admit I love when a bartender has a heavy hand; however, I don't like it the next morning. All things in moderation! I can't blame my bartender friend for hooking me up. I have to blame myself for drinking it too fast and putting myself in the position of wanting another one. Temperance Reversed would say the minute I finish the drink, I should go right back up to the bar for another. You see how the lack of restraint, patience, balance, and moderation can be very bad for you? Advice . . . sip slowly.

# *The*
# MYSTICAL PAIRING

*It takes a good amount of temperance to make a potion work correctly. You must meld the multiple ingredients perfectly to find the balance necessary to create the magic intended. This particular potion is most potent under the light of the morning sun and calls for "hair of the dog." Start the ritual as you would make a traditional Bloody Maria. And call up a few friends and invite them over to magnify the healing qualities of this liquid medicine.*

*Each one of you takes a turn adding an ingredient while saying these magical words, "I accept and value the concept of balance," while going around in a circle until all the ingredients are incorporated. Once completed, pour your individual drinks and add the tiny Coronarita on top, upside down. As you take your first sip, while breathing in the fresh air of the brand-new day, accept the temporary healing properties that this magical potion provides and thank the universe for its boon!*

*Serve in*        *a pint glass*

# *The*
# TEMPERANCE COCKTAIL

---

1 OUNCE SILVER TEQUILA

4 OUNCES CLAMATO OR TOMATO JUICE

3 LIMES, MUDDLED

3 SHAKES WORCESTERSHIRE SAUCE

2 SHAKES SOY SAUCE

4 SHAKES TABASCO

1 TEASPOON SESAME OIL

OLD BAY SEASONING AND SEA SALT

1 ICE-COLD (8-OUNCE) CORONARITA (OR ANOTHER LAGER OF YOUR CHOICE)

1 PICKLED GREEN BEAN, FOR GARNISH

✦

*Fill a cocktail shaker with ice. Add the tequila, Clamato, Worcestershire, soy sauce, Tabasco, and sesame oil into a shaker. Cover and shake until mixed. Place the Old Bay and sea salt on a plate. Press the rim of a chilled pint glass into the mixture to rim the edge. Strain the mixture into the glass. Once combined, pour the beer on top. Garnish with the pickled green bean.*

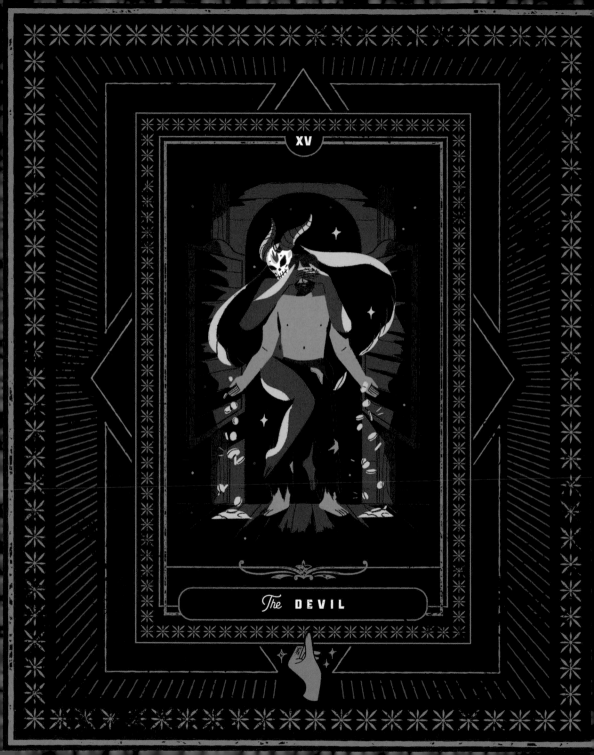

✳✳✳✳✳✳✳✳✳✳✳✳✳✳✳✳✳✳✳✳✳✳✳✳✳✳✳✳✳✳✳✳✳✳✳

## BASIC DEFINITION

The Devil card speaks of vices, addiction, and materialism—all or anything that we put our energies into that may not be the smartest choices for our spiritual growth. What is holding you back from being your true best self? You may not see it now, but these things enslave you and force you to lie to yourself. How easy is it for you to submit to temptation? Can you tell the difference between a healthy versus an unhealthy relationship? When the Devil card pops up in a reading you probably are not aware of the trouble this behavior has been causing you, and the Devil asks if you are strong enough to stop it.

## *Reversed* BASIC DEFINITION

The minute you realize you have an addictive behavior is the first step in doing something about it. The Devil Reversed is all about breaking free of the chains that bind you. It encourages empowerment, release, and freedom from addiction. The Devil Reversed whispers that you are on the verge of something powerful. He may not reveal what it is right away; however, once you see what is holding you back you will finally be liberated. You can take control back in your life and start healing.

## TEQUILA DEFINITION

It's completely fine to have a love for tequila. Having said that, if you find your love is becoming more like an obsession and your relationship to the agave is turning a little too unhealthy and undisciplined, you may want to take a break. Addiction is a real thing that affects many people in the world and should not be taken lightly. Maybe you need to talk to someone about your addiction so you can break free from the chains that bind you and leave this unhealthy relationship. The Devil wants us to keep drinking, but at some point we have to say, "NO!"

## *Reversed* TEQUILA DEFINITION

You think your friends are picking you up for a night of serious drinking and partying but to your surprise they show up at your door, sit you down, and explain how worried they are about you. They force you to see that your drinking has gotten out of control and tell you how much they love you and will support you through recovery. The Devil Reversed says you are ready to face the damage you have been causing yourself and loved ones and are now ready to control the energy that has been controlling you.

# *The* MYSTICAL PAIRING

*You wouldn't let a drink called The Devil stop you from enjoying it, I hope. What if you were feeling a little indulgent this evening and, dare I say, undisciplined? The idea had crossed your mind to submit to some of your vices and allow yourself to give in to temptation. On any typical night you may make a margarita and enjoy the evening and wherever it may take you; however, tonight, your shadow self takes the wheel and you let him. It's one thing to make a delicious drink with your most coveted spirit, tequila. Too bad it's not enough for you on this night. You desire fire, heat, and danger! You reach for the jalapeño-infused tequila and with a sly devilish grin you say, "Why stop there?" Let's add a splash of mezcal for that gentle added kick in the cranium. The remaining ingredients fit like a glove, and while you're content to have just one, you end up making a pitcher. Forgetting momentarily that you are alone, you laugh into the night.*

 *Serve in*  *a double rocks glass*

# *The* DEVIL COCKTAIL

2 OUNCES JALAPEÑO-INFUSED REPOSADO TEQUILA

1/2 OUNCE MEZCAL

1 OUNCE RED PEPPER WATER [JUICED]

1 OUNCE LIME JUICE

1/2 OUNCE AGAVE NECTAR

CRUSHED PINK PEPPERCORNS AND SEA SALT

✦

*Place the tequila, mezcal, pepper water, lime juice, and agave nectar into a shaker with ice. Cover and shake it like you mean it. Place the crushed peppercorns and sea salt on a plate. Press the rim of a chilled double rocks glass into the mixture to rim the edge. Strain the drink into the glass.*

✳✳✳✳✳✳✳✳✳✳✳✳✳✳✳✳✳✳✳✳✳✳✳✳✳✳✳✳✳✳✳✳

## BASIC DEFINITION

The Tower is one of those cards that people dread. The definition of the card means your life is about to change unexpectedly, in some fashion. Usually, the change comes from out of nowhere, and it feels chaotic. Spiritually, your belief system may be challenged, or, on a physical level, you may be faced with a calamity that is unavoidable. The lesson of the Tower is that things have to fall down in order to be built up once again, even sturdier. The Tower makes you stronger and able to handle unavoidable changes that may arise in your future.

## TEQUILA DEFINITION

The club is packed and the music is deafening. Just like any other night, you open up a tab and you start buying yourself and your friends drinks. The night gets away from you and you forget to settle up. Hours later, while at a different location, you realize you don't have your credit card. You look everywhere and retrace your steps, but no one can find it. Always a hard lesson to learn.

## *Reversed* BASIC DEFINITION

The Tower Reversed still points to a big change coming your way with one major difference: You are given enough time and foresight to avoid disaster. Also, look at it this way: Maybe the Tower Reversed is warning you that you are trapped in a holding pattern and your life is not progressing as it should. You may need something to startle you and jump-start your system into finally making the change. At first, this will feel uncomfortable, but eventually it will feel a lot better. Embrace the change!

## *Reversed* TEQUILA DEFINITION

Your good friend challenges you to a drinking contest. First, you think, No way, what am I, still in college? But being a couple drinks in and bored, you get swayed into making this terrible decision. You can foresee the night ending horribly already, but you start going shot for shot. You think by staying hydrated, you could possibly make it through the night unscathed. The Tower Reversed says there's still time to avoid a disaster but you have to let your voice be heard and be adamant about saying no. Your friends will respect you way more for standing your ground than for being a spineless, drunken mess.

THE MAJOR ARCANA

✳

# *The* MYSTICAL PAIRING

*The day may come, and probably has in the past, when you've needed that drink to calm your nerves after experiencing the day you've just had. A day that started like any other . . . until lightning strikes and something big just happened to you. Thinking you will never be the same again, you decide to call a few friends, three to be exact, and you tell them to come over, it's been one of those days.*

*Creating a ritual to clear the wreckage of the Tower is not easy but you insist on trying. This particular ritual must be an abundance of positive energy, generated to balance and counteract the chaos and destruction that has happened to you. The tequila has been infused with rhubarb for a week now and it's ripe for the drinking. The four of you participate in mixing the cocktail. Next, while holding your beverages, say in unison, "I can accept change, I can become change." When completed, throw your glasses into a fireplace and repeat those magic words!*

*Serve in*    *a collins glass*

## _The_
# TOWER COCKTAIL

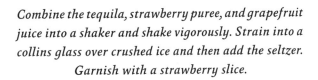

1 1/2 OUNCES RHUBARB-INFUSED BLANCO TEQUILA

1 OUNCE STRAWBERRY PUREE

1 1/2 OUNCES RUBY RED GRAPEFRUIT JUICE

2 OUNCES SELTZER

1 STRAWBERRY SLICE, FOR GARNISH

✦

_Combine the tequila, strawberry puree, and grapefruit juice into a shaker and shake vigorously. Strain into a collins glass over crushed ice and then add the seltzer. Garnish with a strawberry slice._

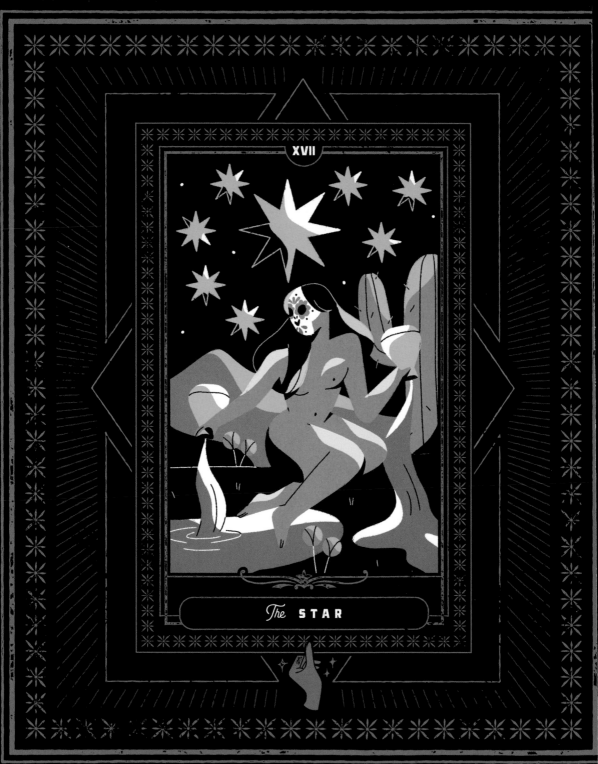

# 17     *The* **STAR**

## BASIC DEFINITION

This magical card speaks of hope, faith, and inspiration. It is the perfect time to make a wish, manifesting an abundance of opportunities to come your way. The universe has your back, so it's time to revitalize and mend those wounds from the past. You are filled with potential; all you have to do is believe in yourself.

## *Reversed* BASIC DEFINITION

You've lost that feeling of hope and inspiration. Instead of rising above the dreary, you are wallowing in the disappointments and failures of your past mistakes and setbacks. Believe in yourself—you are, and have always been, the Star!

## TEQUILA DEFINITION

You're looking forward to a wonderful night out with friends and loved ones. Become inspired after that first group toast and let this magical night sweep you away! Approach the person you're attracted to and offer to buy him or her a drink. Feeling unstoppable and confident, you make a wish for much more to come. Let hope and inspiration guide you on this star-filled night.

## *Reversed* TEQUILA DEFINITION

Self-doubt and lack of confidence stand in your way of having an amazing night. You're lost on the dance floor, dancing alone, feeling spiritually isolated at the bar, without wanting to talk or smile at anyone. You choose to return home in search of a higher purpose instead of being the social butterfly you truly are.

# The
# MYSTICAL PAIRING

*Before starting your star-filled journey, raise your glass and toast the universe and yourself! Bring the glass to your mouth and stop. Pause to smell . . . what is it? Sweetness? Citrus? With your senses wide awake, close your eyes and make a wish. Your fresh new beginning starts right here with innocence, hope, and rejuvenation, one you need only taste to believe in.*

*And just as with your first sip of the elixir, face the rest of the night with the same optimism and wonder.*

*Serve in*     *a double rocks glass*

# _The_
# STAR COCKTAIL

1 1/2 OUNCES SILVER TEQUILA

1/2 OUNCE APEROL

1 OUNCE WATERMELON PUREE

1 OUNCE LEMON JUICE

1/2 OUNCE YUZU AGAVE SYRUP [RECIPE FOLLOWS]

SEA SALT, FOR RIM

1 WATERMELON WEDGE, FOR GARNISH

✦

_Fill a shaker with ice. Add all the ingredients and shake well. Place some sea salt on a plate. Press the rim of a chilled double rocks glass into the sea salt to rim the edge. Strain the mixture into glass with ice. Garnish with the watermelon wedge._

### YUZU AGAVE SYRUP

_Combine 1 cup agave, 1 cup water, and 1/4 ounce yuzu extract in a saucepan and cook over medium heat until you reach a boil. Reduce the heat and reduce until everything melds together. Let chill overnight and keep in the refrigerator for up to two weeks._

# 18

# *The* MOON

✳✳✳✳✳✳✳✳✳✳✳✳✳✳✳✳✳✳✳✳✳✳✳✳✳✳✳✳✳✳✳✳✳✳✳

## BASIC DEFINITION

Everything looks a little bit different under the light of the sugary moon. Things appear creepier. The Moon card speaks of illusion, deception, and unrevealed truths. Is the world hiding a big secret from you? Instead of seeing things at face value, what if you let your imagination and intuition guide you? What if you let your dreams dictate your course of action? What if you weren't meant to know the truth right now? All of these questions come under the light of the moon.

## TEQUILA DEFINITION

The illusion of what we all see when we've had one too many, your deceptive intuition may be telling you the wrong things about the person who just bought you that drink. Don't let your dreams cloud your reality of what's really happening. The psychic self knows what you really want to be doing, and who you want to be doing it with.

## *Reversed* BASIC DEFINITION

A revelation of sorts! Answers start to reveal themselves after you stare into the changing silvery moon for what feels to be days or even weeks. Will you interpret your visions correctly? Now that you are finally starting to get messages, it's important to see through the fog and find your truth. Now, the question is, what will you do with it?

## *Reversed* TEQUILA DEFINITION

Here you may be uncovering a truth, but maybe not the *actual* truth. That realization you have when your hangover wears off and you see who you're lying next to. That awakening or epiphany when you realize you'd rather be home watching television than go somewhere you may later regret. That feeling when you aren't sure if you are the homebody or the party king . . . maybe you're both.

# *The* MYSTICAL PAIRING

*Grab your sage and hurry up!*

*Creating a ritual under the full moon is crafty work. Make some magic through illusion and let your subconscious be your guide. This drink is a ritual in of itself, only the serious and unafraid should attempt its mysterious nature. Through embarking on a meditative path, you will see what is real and what is hidden. When blowing out the candle of the conscious mind all that is left is your dreams . . . where will they lead you? This drink may light your path after a period of darkness and uncertainty.*

*Invite over three close friends to start the ritual. Set the stage with some calming music and light a purple-and-white candle. Have some moonstone, clear quartz, or azurite nearby for helpful illumination. Place a mirror outside a window so it is reflecting the moon inside. As you start drinking your cocktail, stare onto the mirror and say, "Let me see beyond the veil of mystery." Meditate on the sights, sounds, smells, and layers of taste. Open the door to your higher self and unlock the secrets you were always meant to uncover.*

*Serve in*     *a collins glass*

# *The* MOON COCKTAIL

1 OUNCE REPOSADO TEQUILA

1 OUNCE BLANCO TEQUILA

1 OUNCE GUAVA PUREE

3/4 OUNCE ORGEAT [ALMOND FLAVOR]

1 LIME, JUICED

2 DASHES ANGOSTURA BITTERS

LIME SHELL, SOAKED IN 151 RUM

✦

*Place all of the ingredients except the rum-soaked lime shell into a shaker with ice. Cover and shake well. Strain the mixture into a 12-ounce glass with fresh ice. Remove the lime shell from the rum and light it with a match. Once lit, dunk the flame and shell into the glass to extinguish. Place the lime shell on top of the drink and serve.*

XIX

The **SUN**

# 19

# *The* SUN

## BASIC DEFINITION

The Sun is probably the best card to see during a reading. If you ask the tarot a question and the Sun card comes up, the answer is a definite YES! Some of the Sun's most popular definitions are pure joy, love, positivity, birth, and harmony. This card is just what you need to see to start over on the sunny side of the road. Positive vibes are entering your life at this time and you should embrace them. Maybe you'll fall in love with someone beautiful on the inside and outside? If you've been working hard to manifest your dreams and the Sun comes up in your reading, chances are they'll come true.

## *Reversed* BASIC DEFINITION

The Sun Reversed reminds you to look at your glass half full when going through a difficult time. Maybe you feel a little bit like Eeyore. Even when things are going wonderfully in your life, you are prone to looking toward the negative. Why are you drawing clouds into your beautiful sunny picture? When the Sun Reversed shows up in a reading, the universe is telling you to change your negative mindset. You are truly blessed, and, for whatever reason, you are blocking your inspiration and happiness. Maybe you don't feel like you deserve it. That is a crazy thought that you should get rid of immediately.

## TEQUILA DEFINITION

An island getaway with your lover is a great interpretation of the Sun card. If you were to close your eyes and picture your ultimate happy place to holiday, where would it be? Who would you want with you and what would you be drinking? For instance, what ingredients would be in your perfect margarita? Would it taste refreshing and citrusy? Would it look like a photograph on a menu? Whatever it is, have faith that it will be the best darn margarita you've ever had.

## *Reversed* TEQUILA DEFINITION

Your friends have decided to get together and throw you a surprise birthday party. You are truly blessed to have all of these amazing, selfless people in your life who care this much about you. It's unfortunate that you can't enjoy yourself. Instead of toasting with your friends, or laughing about wonderful shared stories, you find yourself getting down about getting older. You can't just allow yourself to see what's right in front of you, and that is how loved you are.

# *The*
# MYSTICAL PAIRING

*The Sun is a welcome sight! After a long night wracked with fear and insecurities you embrace the warmth on your face as you would give your child a hug. Having chased away the darkness and watching it evaporate into the corners, you can finally rejoice.*

*Light attracts light! Use this sunny drink to fill your soul with joy, optimism, and new welcoming friendships. Say YES to opportunities both near and far and old and new. Celebrate the start of a brand-new day. Who says you can't drink tequila in the morning? Put down that tired mimosa and try this—a drink as vibrant as your potential!*

*Serve in*     *a wineglass*

# The
# SUN COCKTAIL

1 OUNCE SILVER TEQUILA

2 OUNCES MANGO NECTAR

1/2 LIME, JUICED

4 OUNCES PROSECCO OR SPARKLING WINE

1 BASIL LEAF, FOR GARNISH

✦

*Add the tequila, mango nectar, and lime juice into a shaker filled with ice. Shake and strain into a wineglass without ice. Top with the sparkling wine. Garnish with a spanked basil leaf—clap the basil leaf between your hands to release aromatics.*

XX

JUDGMENT

❋❋❋❋❋❋❋❋❋❋❋❋❋❋❋❋❋❋❋❋❋❋❋❋❋❋❋❋

## BASIC DEFINITION

Can you feel that? You've changed, and seeing the Judgment card appear in your reading proves it. You have arrived at a very powerful, life-altering stage in your progression. And you have to be able to now reflect on your past and allow yourself to move on. The universe is calling on you right now! The angels are blowing their horns, and you need to listen to what they're telling you. However, before you can move on to the next big step in your life, you have to absolve, release, and forgive yourself of your past. You can't take the old you along for the journey.

## *Reversed* BASIC DEFINITION

The universe is clearly calling for you to change your life but you aren't listening. Guess what? That's Judgment Reversed. You're so busy being caught up in your old ways of self-doubt that you are denying yourself and those who love you the experience of seeing what's behind the veil of the real you. Please fight through the indecision that you're feeling about abandoning your current life in order to accept the universe's message of moving on. Don't be afraid to rise like the phoenix in the story of your life!

## TEQUILA DEFINITION

You're trapped between two versions of yourself. Your day job is unfulfilling, so you invest your money into a restaurant/bar as a silent partner and start spending most of your extra time there. After months of learning, you slowly start becoming more involved, and to your surprise, everyone welcomes you. You have come to a crossroads and feel like the universe is giving you an ultimatum. You know what you want to do. You want to say goodbye to the old you and maybe open up your own bar and who knows what else? There's no going backward, though. You have to stop fighting it and embrace the new you.

## *Reversed* TEQUILA DEFINITION

The days of drinking and partying are behind you. You're now feeling a disconnect between who you are and who your friends think you are. The more you continue this way of life, the longer you deny your true calling of becoming the more mature version of yourself. However, before you cut the cord and make the drastic change into adulthood, you have to say goodbye both literally and metaphorically to the old you.

# *The* MYSTICAL PAIRING

*Quiet your mind and pour your drink.*

*Can you hear it? Very soft and quiet yet strong and determined, the universe and your angels are sending you messages! What does everyone else know about you that you don't yet see? Why are you blind to your achievements and abilities? What would you do and how far would you go to know you are on the right path?*

*When self-doubt and mental obstacles cloud your mind, shut it all down and listen. Alone and ready to begin, you embrace your drink as you would your true calling. Light two candles and place the drink between them. Close your eyes and just be. Can you smell the citrus, the honey, and the flower? Let them break away the walls blocking your intuition, and for the first time in a long time, listen to the universe.*

*Serve in*          *a champagne glass*

# *The* JUDGMENT COCKTAIL

2 1/2 OUNCES BAR HILL GIN

1 OUNCE LEMON JUICE

1/2 OUNCE HONEY SIMPLE SYRUP [SEE PAGE 43]

2 OUNCES CALENDULA ICED TEA [RECIPE FOLLOWS]

1 EGG WHITE

1 MARIGOLD PETAL, FOR GARNISH

✦

*Add the gin, lemon juice, honey simple syrup, and calendula iced tea to a shaker with ice and shake vigorously. Strain into an empty shaker and add the egg white. Then, dry shake (shaking the ingredients without the ice) harder than before and strain into a champagne glass. Float the marigold petal on top.*

### CALENDULA ICED TEA

*Add 2 tablespoons dried calendula marigold petals to a saucepan with 1 cup water and boil. Strain out the petals and chill overnight before using. This will keep in the refrigerator for up to two weeks, or enjoy it on its own!*

# 21 The WORLD

✳✳✳✳✳✳✳✳✳✳✳✳✳✳✳✳✳✳✳✳✳✳✳✳✳✳✳✳✳✳✳✳✳✳✳

## BASIC DEFINITION

The World shows up when you have completed a cycle in your life. Unlike some of the other cards that speak of finishing a phase in your life, the World is a happy ending. You are able to sit back and reflect on the positive outcome of your accomplishments. The World can also mean travel. But no matter what, this card means you've grown and have now mastered a new skill. This card can also represent a big event, like a graduation from college or a retirement. In either case, your journey was a success and you should be very proud of your achievements.

## TEQUILA DEFINITION

What would finish off your ultimate tequila experience? You drink it socially at all of the high-end tequila bars. So now what? How about witnessing the literal journey of tequila itself from agave to alcohol. There are vacations to Mexico where you can learn all about your favorite drink. You can participate in tasting sessions and even create your own tequila blend. This sums up the World card for your tequila adventure. Now you know everything you need to know about this delicious alcohol and can look back on it with positivity.

## *Reversed* BASIC DEFINITION

The World Reversed says you're *almost* there. You just need to follow through and overcome the obstacles and frustrations that have been hindering you lately. You can see the finish line. If you gave up now, would you be happy with the outcome of the long journey you've been on? I would think you'd feel that you did not accomplish what you initially set out to achieve. You might have to wait through a delay. Either way, when the World Reversed is in a reading, I still see a positive. What hasn't happened yet will still eventually happen; you just need to stay the course.

## *Reversed* TEQUILA DEFINITION

Another night of drinking has led to some very interesting dreams. It's your senior year of college and you've finished your final exams. While all set to graduate, fear grips you. One paper still needs to be turned in and if it's not, no graduation for you. Waking up in a sweat, you thank God it was only a dream. Having graduated almost fifteen years ago, this dream is making you doubt your maturity. What can you do to find closure and accept that the past is the past?

# The
# MYSTICAL PAIRING

*Who doesn't want the world? What could possibly be holding you back from attaining it? When a chapter of your life has ended and you wish to move on, this is the potion for you.*

*After gathering your ingredients for The World, make a list of everything in your life that has ended or is holding you back. When the drink is properly made and consumption is a mere moment away, strike a match and watch that list burn into the sky along with all things unwanted and unnecessary. Ritualize the end of an era with a drink meant for change.*

*Watch the mist form over the drink and smell the oils from the zest. Drink deep of the port and live like you've always known you could!*

*Serve in* a double rocks glass

## _The_
# WORLD COCKTAIL

1 1/2 OUNCES ANGEL'S ENVY BOURBON

1 1/2 OUNCES CAMPARI

1 OUNCE CARPANO ANTICA FORMULA VERMOUTH

1/2 OUNCE FONSECA RUBY PORT

ORANGE PEEL, FOR GARNISH [FLAME OPTIONAL; SEE PAGE 9]

✦

_Add all the ingredients to a mixing glass with ice. Stir 12 times in each direction until a noticeable layer of condensation has formed on the outside of the glass. Strain into a double rocks glass with a large ice cube sphere or block. Zest the orange over the glass to release the oils. You should see a mist appear over the cocktail._

# _The_ **MINOR** ARCANA

## ✕ ✕ ✕

_What the mezcal are the Minor Arcana?_

The Minor Arcana, unlike the Major Arcana, refers to things that may pop up in your day-to-day life. Things that may not linger long and can often be changed by how well you assert your free will.

Each suit is associated with its own traits and elements:

**WANDS INCLUDE FIRE SIGNS**
Aries, Leo, and Sagittarius; work, energy, and passion.

**CUPS INCLUDE WATER SIGNS**
Cancer, Scorpio, and Pisces; emotions, love, and intuition.

**SWORDS INCLUDE AIR SIGNS**
Gemini, Libra, and Aquarius; communication, action, and intellect.

**PENTACLES INCLUDE EARTH SIGNS**
Taurus, Virgo, and Capricorn; grounded, practical, and financial.

_And what the Casamigos are Court cards?_

The Court cards—Kings, Queens, Knights, and Pages—can be very hard to interpret. This is because they can either refer to people in your life, aspects of your personality, or specific attributes you may need at the time. How will you know the difference? Your intuition.

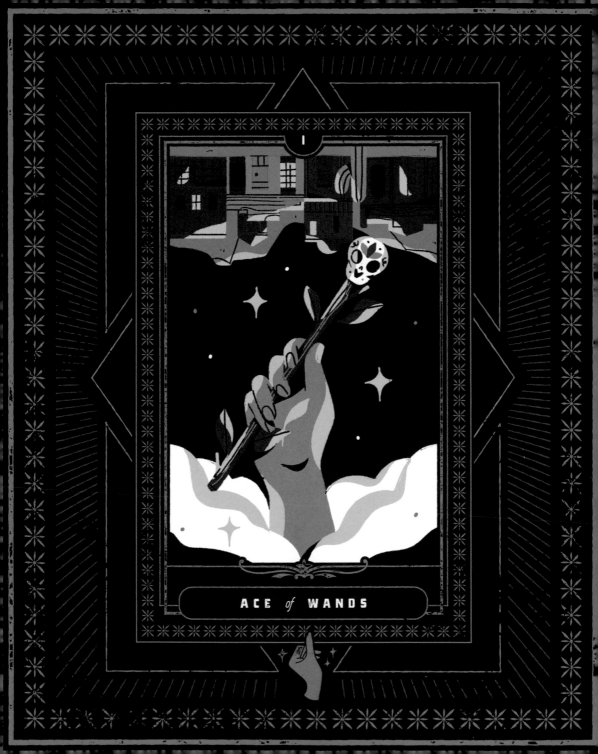

ACE *of* WANDS

# The ACE of WANDS

✳✳✳✳✳✳✳✳✳✳✳✳✳✳✳✳✳✳✳✳✳✳✳✳✳✳✳✳✳✳✳✳✳✳✳✳✳

## BASIC DEFINITION

This fiery card speaks about passionate fresh starts. What is that new idea you have? What are you excited to get underway? You could easily start a new job or enter a new relationship when this card shows up in a reading, depending on the question asked.

## Reversed BASIC DEFINITION

The Ace of Wands Reversed still speaks of new beginnings, but now there are obstacles blocking that energy from igniting. Maybe the start of your new job was postponed? It's possible you're suffering from writer's block and your creative juices are simply not flowing. Don't be overly concerned. Aces are aces, and you're still going to get that burst of positive fiery energy. It may just take a little longer than you would like.

## TEQUILA DEFINITION

The Ace of Wands represents a planned night out, an event you are hosting for work or for fun. Something that's been on the calendar for quite a while that you are super passionate about, such as a concert, first date, or romantic night out at a restaurant you've never been to before.

## Reversed TEQUILA DEFINITION

A night out that you've been really looking forward to is, unfortunately, delayed. A concert gets postponed because the lead singer gets laryngitis. Second thoughts about that first date? Why is that bartender taking so long to serve me my drink?

# MYSTICAL PAIRING

*You better not spend your Saturday night at home! Start your evening with the spice and citrus every good night on the town deserves. Call your friends and invite them on an adventure. Follow your desires and take the path less traveled. Your passionate night of adventure deserves a cocktail that speaks to your heart and opens a new door into a universe, rich with the fire and spark you deserve! Begin your journey right here; just don't burn your tongue.*

*Invite three friends to your house before your night on the town. Once these cocktails are made, light four red candles. While seated near your respective candle, take turns voicing your expectations and desires for the night ahead. Once you've all completed your individual turns, everyone say together, "I am the night," and blow out your candles. Now finish your cocktails and have a night to remember!*

*Serve in* *a double rocks glass*

# *The*
# ACE OF WANDS COCKTAIL

---

### 2 OUNCES GHOST PEPPER TEQUILA

### 3 OUNCES FRESH SQUEEZED TANGERINE JUICE OR ORANGE JUICE

### 3/4 OUNCE HOUSE OF CARDS GRENADINE [RECIPE FOLLOWS]

✦

*Pour the tequila and juice into a double rocks glass
with ice and stir. Top with the grenadine.*

#### HOUSE OF CARDS GRENADINE

*Put equal parts pomegranate juice and cane sugar into a small saucepan.
Cook over medium heat and stir until the sugar is dissolved. Remove from
the heat. Let chill overnight and keep in the refrigerator for up to two weeks.*

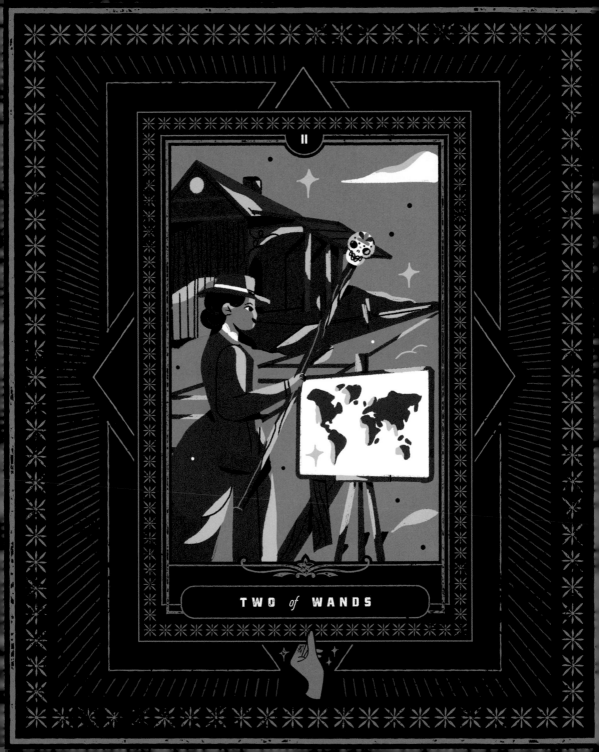

TWO *of* WANDS

# The **TWO** of **WANDS**

✳✳✳✳✳✳✳✳✳✳✳✳✳✳✳✳✳✳✳✳✳✳✳✳✳✳✳✳✳✳✳✳✳

## BASIC DEFINITION

When the Two of Wands shows up in a reading, be ready to make some choices and explore the prospects that you have laid out ahead of you. You have wonderful energy and you are very optimistic about all of the possibilities you have in your future. This card indicates that you have started the groundwork on a new idea or job opportunity and it's looking very positive. You may not have actively started the work yet; however, you know what you have to do in order to be very successful. You may need to step outside your comfort zone, but that's a small price to pay for success.

## TEQUILA DEFINITION

You're smart and creative, and have amazing ideas! You've received multiple job offers, and all you need now is to decide where you will end up. Should you accept the job in the city just an hour away from your family or take the job in Paris? The possibilities are endless, and the world is in your hands. All you have to do now is pull the trigger. Later that night, in order to celebrate, you pull out the really good bottle of reposado that you've been saving for a rainy day to help you decide.

## *Reversed* BASIC DEFINITION

The Two of Wands Reversed says that you are feeling a little insecure and possibly even doubting your potential. The decisions you need to be making right now to further your life's goals are being put on hold by nothing more than your fear. You are so worried about not measuring up against the competition, you remain stuck. No one likes or wants their lives to be placed on hold or be put upon a shelf. Have faith that you can do whatever you put your mind to.

## *Reversed* TEQUILA DEFINITION

You've applied for a bartending job at the hottest new place in town. You've made it past the first round of cuts and now the owner is telling you and five other applicants to make the most perfect margarita he's ever tasted. You are all standing next to each other behind the bar, ready with your ingredients, and you hesitate. You are suddenly questioning your abilities, having seen what the competition has brought to the table. You should feel way more confident than you are. You have been very successful in the past, and you were even approached by the owner to apply. What could go wrong? You got this! Don't let your fears hold you back.

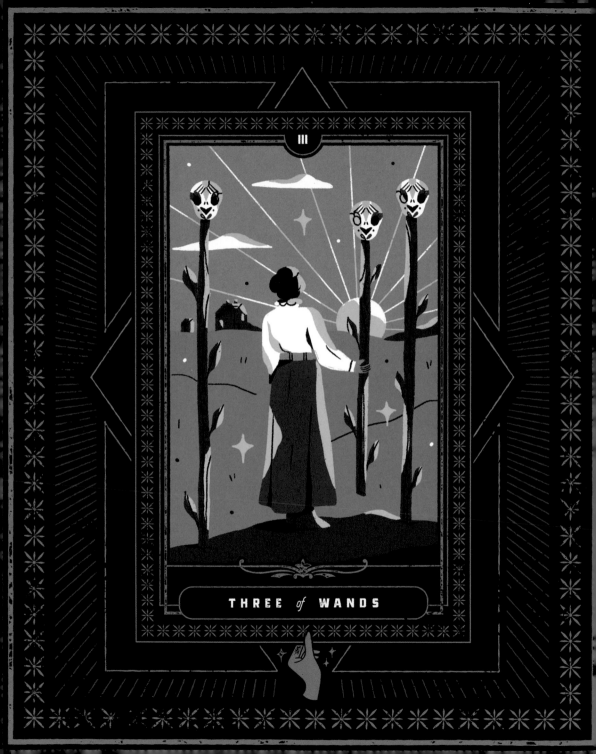

THREE *of* WANDS

# *The* THREE *of* WANDS

## BASIC DEFINITION

The Three of Wands is one of my favorite cards to show up in a reading! This card foretells success through a focused effort. The Three of Wands is what every businessperson wants to see in his or her reading. The card indicates that your energy will present itself into great things. There may be a business expansion that could lead to progress in your career or an actual journey across water. One thing to remember: When the Three of Wands appears, whatever you are working on will be continuously improved upon until it brings the success desired.

## *Reversed* BASIC DEFINITION

When the Three of Wands Reversed appears in front of you, be prepared to face some obstacles or delays in your path to victory. Maybe you are your own worst enemy and lack the confidence to make it big? Or perhaps, you're not working hard enough or dreaming big enough to make your wishes come true? Some people when interpreting the Three of Wands Reversed still say good things are on their way—however, they are just delayed.

## TEQUILA DEFINITION

Through strength, hard work, and dedication you have managed to graduate college and immediately land the job of your dreams. Your friends think you got lucky. But you know that it was because you were very persistent and dedicated to getting hired by this company. On the interviews, you were positive, and your focused energy manifested into exactly the right kind of personality your employers needed to see from you. As your friends are toasting you with a round of tequila shots, you realize that your hard work has paid off and with it comes the arrival of opportunities.

## *Reversed* TEQUILA DEFINITION

Starting your own bar/restaurant with friends has been your dream since college. You have worked so hard to get to where you need to be and even managed to trust a few individuals to share ownership with. Even though your ducks are all in a row, your partners still have obstacles and delays to work through. This frustration and fear is, unfortunately, making you doubt whether or not this will ever happen. You know deep down it will. But still, the work thus far has gone unrewarded. Hopefully, it'll start picking up steam.

# The
# MYSTICAL PAIRING

There is nothing out of the ordinary about toasting a new venture, enterprise, or partnership. As a matter of fact, I think it's a great idea! Celebrate all the hard work you have already put in, making sure that moving forward will be a grand success.

If you are going to toast your future financial success, make sure you're utilizing the right cocktail. Champagne will not do the trick. You need a beverage with a hint of spice and creativity! One that is worthy of all the hard work that led to this win.

The perfect drink for the businessperson and entrepreneur, the Three of Wands is best when toasted with business partners upon completion of a goal. It's not enough to just celebrate your successes with words. To give something more power, include a physical component to help manifest it into the material world. As you raise your glass with your associates, congratulate each other and visualize the victory. When you take your first sip, take three gulps!

*Serve in* a double rocks glass

# *The*
# THREE OF WANDS COCKTAIL

1 1/2 OUNCES REPOSADO TEQUILA

1/2 OUNCE EL BUHO MEZCAL

1 OUNCE LEMON JUICE

1 OUNCE HOT HONEY SYRUP (RECIPE FOLLOWS)

BLACK SEA SALT, FOR RIM

LEMON ZEST, FOR GARNISH

FRESHLY GROUND BLACK PEPPER, FOR GARNISH

✦

*Shake all the ingredients together with ice. Pour some black sea salt in a small dish. Dip a chilled double rocks glass into the salt to rim the glass. Add some ice and pour the cocktail into the rimmed glass. Garnish with the lemon zest and pepper.*

### HOT HONEY SYRUP

*Put 1/2 cup hot honey, 1/2 cup water, 1 teaspoon turmeric, and 1 teaspoon ground black pepper into a small saucepan and cook over medium heat until combined. Let chill overnight and keep in the refrigerator for up to two weeks.*

IV

FOUR *of* WANDS

# The FOUR of WANDS

✳✳✳✳✳✳✳✳✳✳✳✳✳✳✳✳✳✳✳✳✳✳✳✳✳✳✳✳✳

## BASIC DEFINITION

The Four of Wands is a joyous card that foretells a celebration or shared achievement/milestone, such as a romantic getaway to celebrate a wedding anniversary. It can also point to a party someone is throwing for you that will bring together many individuals who love you. When this card shows up in a reading, I cannot help but see the happiness jump out! If you ask the tarot a question such as "Will they propose?" or "Are they interested in me?" the answer would be a definite yes!

## *Reversed* BASIC DEFINITION

When such a beautiful card shows up reversed, that special little getaway you and your lover had planned might be postponed. The Four of Wands Reversed can mean that an upheaval or uncertainty got thrown your way and is now temporarily blocking your happiness. Never fear, though: your time in the sun will still happen. It just might happen a little further down the road.

## TEQUILA DEFINITION

All of the months spent planning your wedding have come to this very moment. You're so happy you can't contain yourself! It's time for the best man to give the toast, and you sit back and brace yourself. You're expecting an embarrassing story or something that will get everyone laughing. Instead, your friend surprises you with such a nice, warmhearted speech that it brings tears to yours and the room's eyes. What a wonderful way to get married, together, with your new spouse, in a room full of people who truly love and want the best for you both. So what if you insisted the champagne toast be a tequila shot instead?

## *Reversed* TEQUILA DEFINITION

A couple wants to go to Bermuda to celebrate their ten-year anniversary but they just can't seem to make it happen. They've put their romantic vacation on hold for months now. And they're worried it may never happen. The idea of margaritas on the beach and feet in the sand is almost enough to get them through the day-to-day nonsense. But the trip needs to *actually* happen. Getting caught up in the drama of everyday life can really carry you away if you let it. They begin to laugh about all the obstacles that have gotten in the way and finally book the trip!

# MYSTICAL PAIRING

*Are you planning a trip with someone special? If so, start preparing the ingredients for this cocktail ahead of time. It takes ten days to make the homemade fennel liqueur and you don't want to rush it, just like you wouldn't want to rush your vacation.*

*The night before your weekend getaway, come together as one and share in this magical drink. Allow yourselves to be as connected in every way. Experience your love for each other as if for the first time. Acknowledge your senses while getting caught up in the rapture. Let yourselves get carried away!*

*With empty glasses, stare into each other's eyes and promise out loud that you will both have the most positive experience together imaginable. Seal it with a kiss, and maybe another.*

*Serve in*     *a champagne glass*

## *The*
# FOUR OF WANDS COCKTAIL

---

### 1 1/2 OUNCES PAPA'S PILAR RUM

### 1 OUNCE HOMEMADE FINOCCHIETTO LIQUEUR [RECIPE FOLLOWS]

### 1 OUNCE FRESH LEMON JUICE

### 1 OUNCE FRESH GRAPEFRUIT JUICE

### 1/2 OUNCE HONEY SIMPLE SYRUP [SEE PAGE 43]

### 1 EGG WHITE [OPTIONAL]

### 2 FENNEL SEEDS [OPTIONAL; FOR GARNISH]

✦

*Fill a cocktail shaker with ice. Add all the ingredients and shake. Strain the mixture into a champagne glass without ice. If you decide to add the egg white (and I hope you do), garnish with a couple fennel seeds. The egg white will add froth.*

#### HOMEMADE FINOCCHIETTO LIQUEUR

*Add 10 fennel seeds to 1/2 cup moonshine in a quart container and let sit for 10 days. Add 1/2 cup of simple syrup and let sit for a day. Shake the container. Congratulations! You just made your own fennel liqueur. Keep it in the fridge for up to two weeks.*

FIVE *of* WANDS

# *The* FIVE *of* WANDS

❊❊❊❊❊❊❊❊❊❊❊❊❊❊❊❊❊❊❊❊❊❊❊❊❊❊❊❊❊❊❊❊❊❊

## BASIC DEFINITION

The Five of Wands warns of challenge and competition. When this card shows itself in a reading, be prepared for obstacles. You may also want to make sure your energy is fully charged before you tackle your goals. The Five of Wands can mean a problematic day where nothing is easy to accomplish. Or it can be everything, and everyone is pushing you to your limits, so you have to up your game to be the winner. Sometimes nothing is easy, and it really comes down to your perseverance and ability to harness the chaos around you and make it work for you, not against you.

## *Reversed* BASIC DEFINITION

The Five of Wands Reversed confirms that there will be problems heading your way but that instead of charging at them headfirst, you are taking the passive approach and looking for ways to avoid the conflict. The Five of Wands Reversed also asks, Why do you need to compete when you can collaborate instead? Maybe it is time for a truce and compromise instead of being overly competitive? Regardless, use this card to think about the best course of action before you make any decisions you may regret.

## TEQUILA DEFINITION

Some people drink to escape, but what they find out eventually is that it only brings on a myriad of other unexpected issues. Now, you aren't thinking clearly, and what would normally be a regular run-of-the-mill, problematic day is now made worse by tequila, a beverage that should be enjoyed responsibly. It shouldn't be used for problem-solving or to surpass your limits. The Five of Wands is unstable and chaotic; the last thing you need is to be buzzed!

## *Reversed* TEQUILA DEFINITION

Why do your friends have to be so damn competitive about everything? Whether it's playing baseball or looking to meet women at bars, it's annoying. It's like you having to be at your best all of the time, which is exhausting. You want so badly to be able to work as a team instead of always against each other. You try to buy a round of shots to foster some camaraderie, but it only leads to everyone else insisting on buying a round until you're all too drunk to think clearly. Not the way you wanted the night to end.

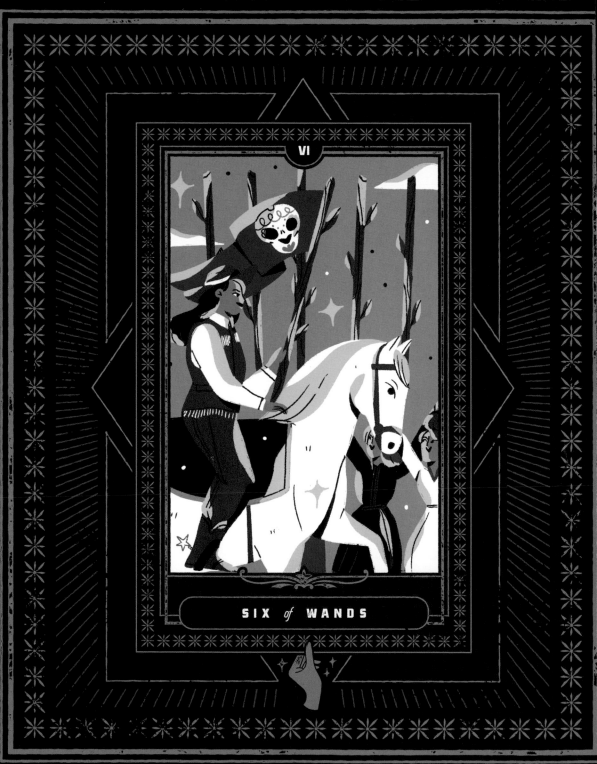

# The SIX of WANDS

## BASIC DEFINITION

The Six of Wands shouts success and leadership! You've just won a big victory and your optimism and popularity inspires everyone you meet. You are being acknowledged for your abilities and possibly rewarded for them as well. When this card shows up in a reading, think about how you're handling your accomplishments, and how that is seen by those around you. This is your time to shine, so handle it the right way!

## *Reversed* BASIC DEFINITION

Where the Six of Wands talks of success and popularity, the Six of Wands Reversed indicates your fear of failure and/or people seeing you fall from grace. Whether it's excessive pride, pessimism, or a major loss, it is now time to rebuild your reputation and start from scratch. You may have been publicly disgraced or failed at something you should have excelled at. Take the time to understand why you ended up this way and learn from it. Don't let your ego take a major hit. Everyone, from time to time, feels the same way as you do right now, and it won't last.

## TEQUILA DEFINITION

You're not just a bartender, you're a mixologist! You've appeared in articles and are the actual face of the bar where you've made a name for yourself over the past five years. You train all the new employees and have the owner wrapped around your finger. People from all over make a point to stop in to see what new concoctions you are making, and you never disappoint. They are not merely drinks but works of art. You are now at a place where people aspire to be like you. It's not like you need the public validation, but you'll admit it doesn't hurt either.

## *Reversed* TEQUILA DEFINITION

Getting thrown out of a bar for fighting last night wasn't entirely your fault. Sure, you defended someone's honor, but the bouncers didn't see it that way. All they witnessed was your jumping over a table like an animal and punching some clown in the face. That got you booted from your favorite watering hole, never to return. It's heartbreaking how one bad day can change everyone's perception of you; you really liked the place, and all the employees knew you there. It takes a lot of courage, but you call the owner to apologize. You tell your side of the story and ask for forgiveness. Reluctantly, you are allowed back. It looks like you'll be on your best behavior for a while.

# The SEVEN of WANDS

## BASIC DEFINITION

The Seven of Wands reinforces that you are in a position of power; however, when you get to be the king of the mountain, you need to be prepared to stand your ground and attack those who want what you now have. This card is all about protecting yourself and taking a defensive stand. You must remember that you have the high ground in this scenario and that everyone trying to knock you off your position of power is at a disadvantage. You must always be ready to protect yourself once you have achieved something others desperately want. You must have unshakable determination and willpower to hold your ground and you will.

## TEQUILA DEFINITION

You're the number one tequila company on the market today. You didn't get that way because of luck. Many smaller companies and ones backed by likeable celebrities want what you have and are trying to get it. You have something they don't, though: You have the experience and the household name. The good news is, you're not going anywhere. The bad news is you can never allow yourself to become overly comfortable either.

## *Reversed* BASIC DEFINITION

Just like with the Seven of Wands, your competitors, or those who envy you, are still coming at you. But with this reversed energy you're being faced with, the feeling to give up or throw in the cards is weighing on you. You may feel as though you aren't ready to properly defend yourself or that the odds are stacked up against you. It's possible that your lack of preparedness and hesitation may make you feel like you are going to lose, but it's just your perception and you still have the upper hand. Just make sure you are defending yourself from the right people because even your friends may want a piece of what you have.

## *Reversed* TEQUILA DEFINITION

It's okay to feel a little defensive and territorial when you're dating the most attractive and popular bartender around. Feelings of paranoia overcome you as you question if everyone is staring at you, judging. The last thing you need is an attack on your ego. Don't let the gawkers see the apprehension and hesitation that you are trying so hard to suppress. The bartender is dating you and you need to own that! Now is not the time to retreat and show your insecurities.

EIGHT *of* WANDS

# The EIGHT of WANDS

✳✳✳✳✳✳✳✳✳✳✳✳✳✳✳✳✳✳✳✳✳✳✳✳✳✳✳✳✳✳✳

## BASIC DEFINITION

When your life seems to be picking up speed, you may be feeling the energy of the Eight of Wands. This card is all about positive movement. It could pertain to travel or love, or receiving good news. The Eight of Wands could also mean that something you have been working on for quite some time might be finally progressing. Expect rapid action in your life! Imagine that you are the wands in this card being propelled into the air, moving as fast as you can. That's the feeling of the Eight of Wands.

## *Reversed* BASIC DEFINITION

The Eight of Wands Reversed can mean two very opposing things. One definition has to do with frustration, delays, and life slowing down. The other definition could mean that you are rushing through something that needs or demands your time. Maybe you're impatient or feeling burnt out? It's possible you want something in your life to speed up so badly your energy becomes unfocused and unstable. How will you accomplish anything feeling that way?

## TEQUILA DEFINITION

Your favorite tequila company is having a contest. You jumped at the chance to participate; after all, the winner gets an all-expenses-paid vacation to Mexico to visit their tequila distillery. You thought the likelihood of actually winning would be next to zero. However, when you received the "You won!" notification, you were off to the races and everything seemed to move at lightning speed. The vacation was amazing but went so fast, it felt like it was over before it even began. This unexpected positive news was just what the doctor ordered to get you through a recent rough patch you may have encountered.

## *Reversed* TEQUILA DEFINITION

You can't force someone to understand you when you've clearly had too much tequila. You're all over the place and completely overbearing. An argument has already started and instead of trying to talk it out, like a rational person, you are making matters worse by rushing with your words. It's not helping that your energy is like lightning that bounces off everyone whom you come into contact with. Maybe you should just go home before the wands in the air explode into combustible flames and burn everything down.

NINE *of* WANDS

✳✳✳✳✳✳✳✳✳✳✳✳✳✳✳✳✳✳✳✳✳✳✳✳✳✳✳✳✳✳✳

## BASIC DEFINITION

The Nine of Wands defines a time when you are so close to finishing the battle that you need to buckle down and focus on the final push. This card represents courage and standing up and fighting, even though the obstacles in your way may be great in size. This card speaks of your reserved strength and not giving up even though you feel like your tank is almost empty. During this time of battle, remind yourself that you are almost at the finish line and you just need to rely on faith and perseverance to get you through the last stretch.

## *Reversed* BASIC DEFINITION

The Nine of Wands Reversed teaches a lesson that says the only way forward is to let go of the past and forgive yourself and/or others. Don't waste any more energy dwelling on a situation that is over. Once you open up to trust and new love, there will be fewer obstacles in front of you. The war is and has been over for some time. So why are you still fighting it? Allow yourself to move on and heal.

## TEQUILA DEFINITION

You've spent a good portion of your life coming to terms with whether or not you have a drinking problem. When you finally decide to go cold turkey and attend meetings, you are excited to welcome the new you who would evolve, hopefully sooner than later. You're a veteran drinker who has seen your fair share of battle scars. Now that you have the courage and faith necessary to stand up to your problem, you have to maintain this dedication and newfound resilience. The hard part is over, now's the time to start your life!

## *Reversed* TEQUILA DEFINITION

You never thought you'd get over your best friend hooking up with your partner. It was a horrible time in your life when you did not want to go out anymore or trust people. That nefarious deed cost you two valuable friendships, and now you have the emotional battle scars to prove it. The resentment you've been battling with has consumed you. Impeded by your own sadness, you have been unable to move forward onto anything new and positive, until recently. You had to learn to let go and accept that you can't control everything, especially what two people do behind your back.

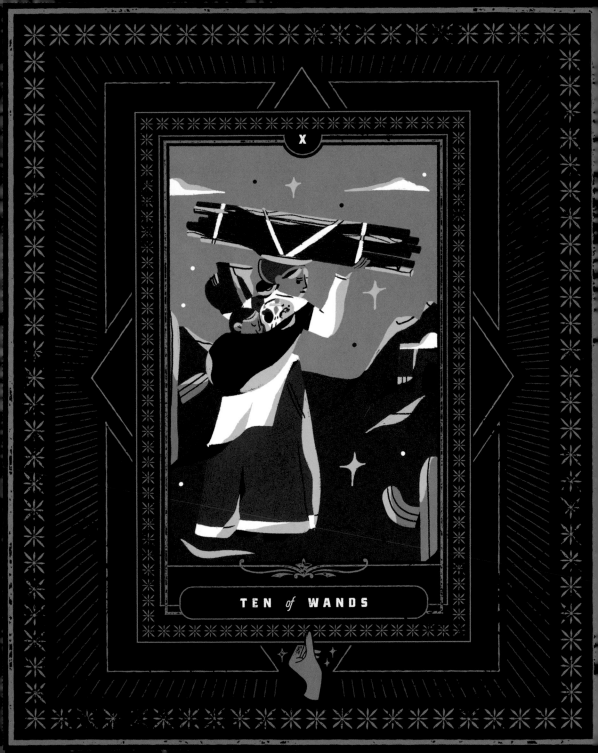

X

TEN *of* WANDS

# The TEN of WANDS

## BASIC DEFINITION

The Ten of Wands is a card many people can relate to. The main takeaways from this card are responsibility, taking on too much yourself, and the stress that comes along with it. The Ten of Wands carries the message to keep going, no matter how heavy the weight you are bearing. You may not realize it, but you are nearing the final stretch. Maybe to help yourself, you can prioritize what is most important and take on those tasks first. Also, why do you feel the need to take on all this burden or accountability all by yourself? Do you think if you don't do all that is needed to get done, no one will? Or, maybe you feel no one can do it as good as you?

## TEQUILA DEFINITION

All your friends rely on you to do most of the work when it comes to entertaining. You laugh to yourself, as you realize, it's been like this for as long as you can remember. Are you that much of a control freak? You offer to host the party as usual and with it comes most of the cooking. Sure, people ask if they can contribute but you never let them. Maybe you secretly like knowing that you are in control and prefer it, even though the stress and pressure of taking on all of the extra responsibility makes you anxious.

## *Reversed* BASIC DEFINITION

The Ten of Wands Reversed still speaks of overburdening yourself like its upright counterpart; however, the reason why may be different. Is your energy and attention being divided so you can't focus on completing a single task? Are people forcing you into doing more than your fair share? Or maybe you have difficulty asking for help. This card warns that when you carry too many things you risk dropping them. Also, after a while, you will start resenting those who aren't helping you, and you may start cutting ties or breaking away from those taking advantage.

## *Reversed* TEQUILA DEFINITION

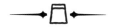

Just because you don't drink as much as your friends do doesn't mean you appreciate being thrown into the designated driver role every time you go out. Your friends don't even seem to ask you anymore. They just assume you will take on all the responsibility all the time. It's starting to really upset you and you start thinking about ways to get out of hanging out with them. You really need to stand up for yourself and be honest about how it makes you feel. You also need to reevaluate how you got to be in this situation in the first place.

PAGE *of* WANDS

# *The* PAGE *of* WANDS

✳✳✳✳✳✳✳✳✳✳✳✳✳✳✳✳✳✳✳✳✳✳✳✳✳✳✳✳✳✳✳✳✳

## BASIC DEFINITION

The Page of Wands brings a positive and encouraging message. It can also mean that you are creative, optimistic, and a free spirit or that you know a younger person who has these attributes. The Page of Wands can show up in a reading when you have a fresh, new idea and/or a newly found inspiration and want to shout it to the world. This fiery Page can also indicate that you will be returning to something that at one time gave you pleasure, but for whatever reason you gave it up. Now might be the perfect time to begin it again.

## TEQUILA DEFINITION

Sometimes you have to just get in your car and drive! Out of nowhere, your friend who lives across the country invites you to stay with them for a week and you answer with an enthusiastic "YES!" Being the free spirit that you are, you pack a small bag that includes a toothbrush, a change of clothes, and a bottle of tequila. This exciting adventure is just what you need to get your creative juices pumping again. Maybe now you can finish that book you keep putting off.

## *Reversed* BASIC DEFINITION

Unfortunately, the Page of Wands Reversed can bring a message of bad news. It can also mean a delay of your plans due to indecision or lack of desire. Anything that can take the wind out of your sails might be connected to the Page of Wands Reversed. It could mean a child is acting out by being rebellious—maybe by having too much of a good time and not concentrating on schoolwork.

## *Reversed* TEQUILA DEFINITION

After graduation from college or grad school, your lack of desire and focus are creating obstacles to landing a new job right away, which is upsetting both you and your parents, because unfortunately that means you will be moving back in with them until you can get your energy going in the right direction. Maybe you've been drinking a little too much and that's making you feel down on yourself. No matter how long the delay, you must remain confident that you will soon attain that new job and start the much-anticipated next chapter of your life.

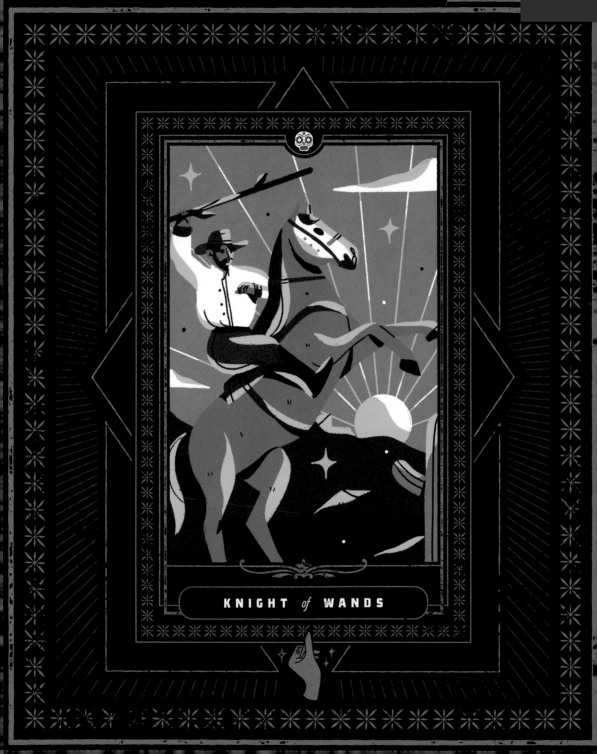

KNIGHT *of* WANDS

# The **KNIGHT** of **WANDS**

✳✳✳✳✳✳✳✳✳✳✳✳✳✳✳✳✳✳✳✳✳✳✳✳✳✳✳✳✳✳✳✳

## BASIC DEFINITION

When the Knight of Wands charges into your reading, be ready to go on a journey! Whether it's to pursue your dreams or just to change your residence or job, no one will ever say the Knight of Wands is being lazy. The person the Knight of Wands represents is one of charisma, passion, and a fiery personality. They are risk-takers and very loyal to their friends and loved ones. This card makes me think of Tigger from *Winnie-the-Pooh*—a constant source of electric energy that may be a bit too impulsive, but their positivity makes up for it.

## *Reversed* BASIC DEFINITION

The Knight of Wands Reversed can be very reckless in nature and rarely, if ever, looks before they leap. The reversed Knight can be unreliable and impatient, not to mention completely narcissistic. If someone is interested in learning about their partner in a relationship and this card popped up, I would caution that this person may be out for just some fun and not take you or the relationship very seriously. If this card represents you as the person being read, then you should try to focus more to become self-aware of what seems to be getting in your way or holding you back. Sometimes, it's fair to say, people like calm energy, not erratic.

## TEQUILA DEFINITION

You're the person who knows what they want and you go out and get it. You are so excited to apply for a job that you forget to bring your résumé to the interview. The look on your prospective employer's face is one of shock and disbelief, but he loved you anyway. Fast-forward a year into the job. You are a trusted part of the team and such a bolt of positivity that everyone, including your direct manager, appreciates having you on the team. The pricey bottle of añejo they gifted you for your one-year anniversary was a nice touch.

## *Reversed* TEQUILA DEFINITION

You so badly want to be her Knight in shining armor, but the problem is, she has one already and he's far from shining. As a matter of fact, his armor is tarnished and so is his behavior. What does she see in him, you wonder? You can tell he doesn't really care about her, he only cares about himself, and instant gratification. One day, you think, you'll be brave enough to approach her. If only you knew she respects this type of bold behavior.

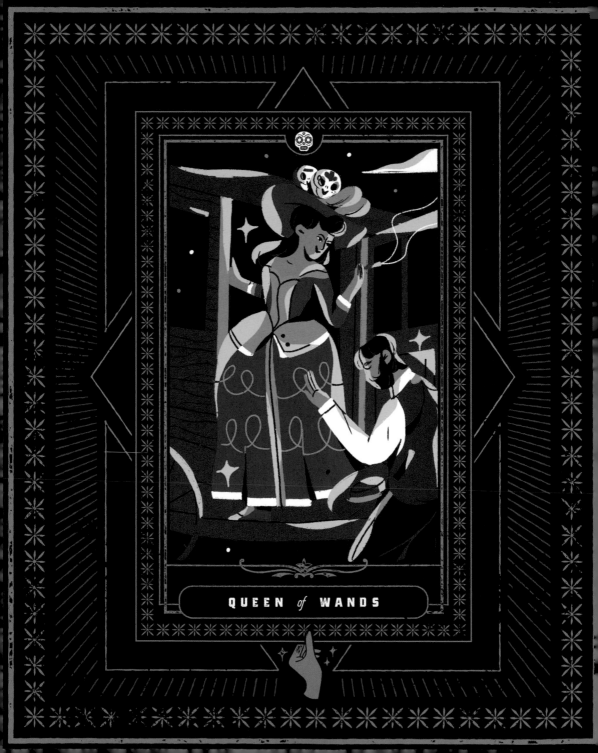

QUEEN of WANDS

# The QUEEN of WANDS

✳✳✳✳✳✳✳✳✳✳✳✳✳✳✳✳✳✳✳✳✳✳✳✳✳✳✳✳✳✳✳✳✳✳

## BASIC DEFINITION

The Queen of Wands is a strong, passionate woman or man who embodies many of the qualities that make for a great person of influence. Many a person would love to marry the Queen of Wands! She's a positive beacon of light that will never burn out on you. When this card shows up in your reading, you are truly being your best self. It can refer to your marriage or work, but whatever it is, you've got everything under control and are loved. Instead of being feared by everyone who reports to you, you are their fierce and loyal leader.

## Reversed BASIC DEFINITION

When the Queen of Wands Reversed makes her entrance, be prepared to tread lightly. She has the negative traits that are opposite to her upright counterpart. If in a leadership role, she is not as vocal, and would rather keep things to herself than to lead her troops to victory. Maybe they're too overly involved with themselves to care enough about anyone else for the time being. It's also very possible that the reversed Queen might not be passionate about a person or project that they previously felt strongly about. This Queen can also be looking for a fight and might not mind that they are feared more than loved.

## TEQUILA DEFINITION

You are more than aware that some restaurants have both good and bad qualities. At this particular location, the food is hit or miss; however, the server is on point. Not only does this person bring your tequila right away, they genuinely make you feel good. There is a possibility it could be all for a good tip, but you don't buy it. You know in your heart this level of authenticity can't be faked.

## Reversed TEQUILA DEFINITION

When she drinks, the Queen of Wands Reversed becomes a bit of a problematic girlfriend. She's not the most trusting on the dance floor, and you hate that you have to keep an eye on her. She doesn't trust you at all, but God forbid you question her motives outwardly. She can also be a bit argumentative and, dare you say, deceitful? No, that's probably too strong a word; however, if the shoe fits . . . The worst part of the situation is that she's not always like this. When she's not drinking, she is the loveliest person you know. It's just on those nights when she loses control, you question the relationship.

# *The*
# MYSTICAL PAIRING

*We are all on a journey of growth and achievement. Along this journey we may get stuck and question our abilities. When thinking about self-improvement, imagine the person you want to be, and hold that image in your mind. Personality traits like charisma, generosity, independence, and confidence are all within your grasp. You just need to believe!*

*This cocktail will make you want to become the person you truly aspire to be. The sweet and spicy juxtaposed by the citrus will subtly remind you of how dynamic you really are. You are as sweet as honey, as spicy as a jalapeño, and as grounded as the earthiness that you can find in mezcal. Embrace your many layers and show the world you are more than meets the eye.*

*The ritual associated with this drink is as follows:*

*Put on a song that makes you feel powerful.*

*Wear an outfit that makes you feel beautiful.*

*Drink the cocktail and embrace the feeling.*

*Hold on to all you're experiencing at that minute. And when all three things are at their zenith and you can barely stand it anymore, yell out to the universe, "I am the Queen of Wands!"*

*Serve in*     *a coupe glass*

# _The_ QUEEN OF WANDS COCKTAIL

1 1/2 OUNCES JALAPEÑO-INFUSED TEQUILA

1/2 OUNCE EL BUHO MEZCAL

1 OUNCE RASPBERRY ALMOND HONEY SYRUP [RECIPE FOLLOWS]

2 OUNCES FRESH LEMON JUICE

1/2 OUNCE GARBANZO BEAN WATER, FOR FROTH

1 RASPBERRY, FOR GARNISH

✦

_Fill a cocktail shaker with ice and add all the ingredients. Shake vigorously and strain into a coupe glass without ice. Garnish with a sworded raspberry._

### RASPBERRY ALMOND HONEY SYRUP

_Add 1 pint of raspberries to a saucepan with 1 cup water and 1 cup honey. Cook over medium heat, stirring constantly so the raspberries break apart. Reduce the heat and add two drops of almond extract and one drop of vanilla extract. Pour the syrup through a double strainer to remove the seeds. Chill overnight and keep in the refrigerator for up to two weeks._

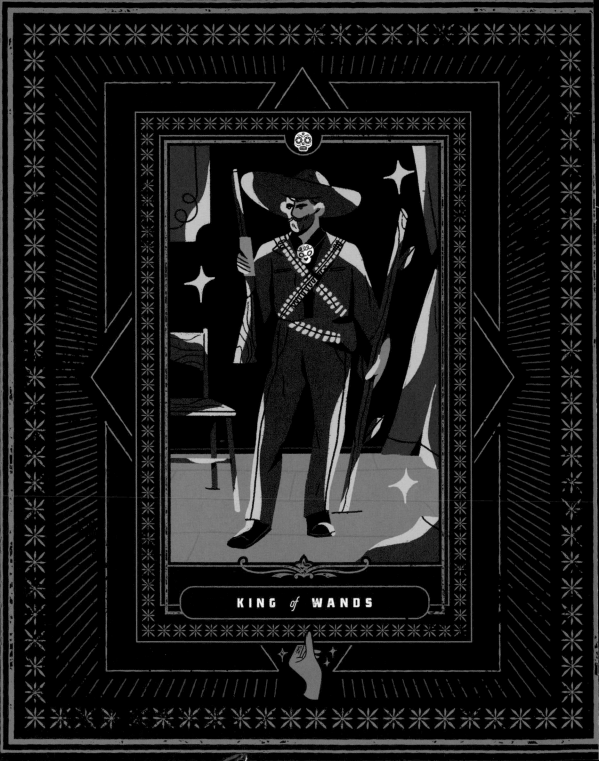

KING *of* WANDS

# The KING of WANDS

## BASIC DEFINITION

The King of Wands represents and embodies all the most positive traits from the Wands suit. They are natural-born leaders who are both visionary and have a true entrepreneurial spirit. They are the ones who come up with the most creative ideas, and they are very successful because of them. This is the man or woman that you aspire to be. They take good care of their homes and families, as well as their work families. You feel comfortable around the King of Wands and know you can trust them with the most important of matters.

## *Reversed* BASIC DEFINITION

The King of Wands Reversed is more like a shrewd immature dictator than a generous inspirational manager. Their idea of effective managing is very much the opposite of what you like in a leader. They explode in anger when something doesn't go their way and they're such egomaniacs that it's amazing they even notice you are in the same room. If the King of Wands Reversed shows up in a reading and you have a wonderful manager or spouse, then maybe it's referring to an aspect of your personality that you need to work on. Maybe you can be a tad impatient or need to work on your compassion skills. Either way, use this card (or any reversed court card) to learn from and maybe even improve on something about yourself.

## TEQUILA DEFINITION

You turned down a job offer today. When all is said and done, you just can't leave your manager. Obviously, you're not going to hold your life up because of him, but he is just a good person to work for. He's a generous and authentic leader, someone who has a creative spark and a fire within that is infectious. Honestly, he's an inspiration to you and everyone else he works with, not to mention that when you hit your sales goal, he buys you the occasional nice bottle of tequila to celebrate.

## *Reversed* TEQUILA DEFINITION

The company Christmas party was one for the books for sure. It had everything you'd expect, except maybe for the part where the male CEO drank so much that he started hitting on all the female employees. He was doing shots of tequila and intimidating subordinates to do the same. The immature, arrogant display makes you rethink even coming back to work on Monday. Besides his childlike behavior, he's normally an abusive individual to work for anyway.

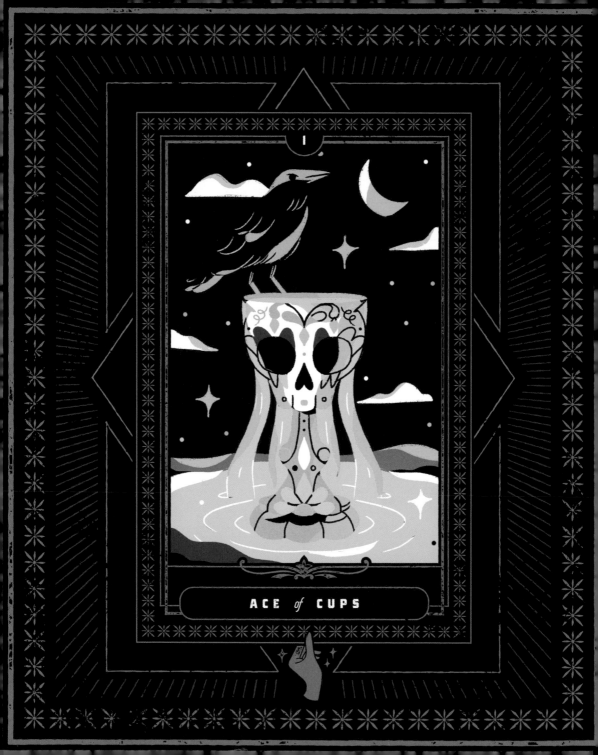

ACE *of* CUPS

# The ACE of CUPS

## BASIC DEFINITION

True love starts from within. The Ace of Cups spouts forth an awakening of the heart. You feel the love flowing within you and you feel the joy that accompanies it. The Ace of Cups can represent any new blossoming love interest, whether it be romantic or friendly. It can refer to the beginning of a new creative idea, a birth of a child, or an engagement. If you ask the tarot any question revolving around love, then the answer is "YES."

## TEQUILA DEFINITION

Who says you can't make a toast with tequila? Why does it have to sparkle? Any special occasion that warrants a glass of your best tequila can be defined as an Ace of Cups moment. A wedding toast, a birth of a child, or a romantic anniversary celebration would all be perfect examples of a magical Ace of Cups moment to remember.

## Reversed DEFINITION

The Ace of Cups Reversed asks if you are allowing yourself to be open to the possibility of love. You may have been through a rough patch with your last relationship, but now you are ready to get back on the horse. Hopefully, you have taken the time to nurture yourself and recover from any emotional damage from your past. When this attractive card shows up in a reading reversed, you're still going to get the beginning you deserve—it just may take a little longer than you hoped.

## Reversed TEQUILA DEFINITION

Why even go out on the blind date if you aren't truly open to starting a new relationship? There you are, margarita in hand, casually engaged in a flirty conversation. The two of you seem to be enjoying each other's company, but you know deep down that you are not ready to be dating yet. It's too bad because this one, you can tell, is a keeper. However, will he/she wait for you when you are eventually ready? Would you ask them to?

# *The* MYSTICAL PAIRING

*Who wouldn't want a new emotional connection? A relationship that is filled with love, compassion, and trust? Shouldn't it be something every one of us should be able to experience?*

*Picture yourself floating adrift in a calm lake, eyes turned to the cloud formations above. You start seeing images, and as you float off into dreams you are here, there, and everywhere. You are a part of the natural flow and want to experience it all.*

*When making the Ace of Cups recipe breathe in the lavender-infused gin and let it relax you. Place a drop of the honey syrup on your tongue as a playful tease of what's soon to follow. Think about the resurrecting properties of the beautiful lotus flower and let it carry your faith to new heights. Let this cocktail be your inspiration to love! Share it with someone you care for and let it do its magic.*

*Serve in*     *a tall stemmed glass*

# *The*
# ACE OF CUPS COCKTAIL

1 1/2 OUNCES LAVENDER-INFUSED GIN

3 OUNCES LOTUS FLOWER ICED TEA [RECIPE FOLLOWS]

5 OUNCES YUZU HONEY SYRUP [SEE PAGE 47]

4 PEPPERMINT LEAVES, RIPPED AND SPANKED

1 SPRIG FRESH MINT, FOR GARNISH

✦

*Place ice in a cocktail shaker. Add all the ingredients,*
*cover, and shake well. Pour into a tall stemmed glass*
*and garnish with the sprig of mint.*

## LOTUS FLOWER ICED TEA

*Wrap 2 cups loose lotus tea leaf in a cheesecloth and place everything in a*
*saucepan with 4 cups water. Bring water to a boil. Remove from the heat*
*and then chill overnight before using. Keep in the refrigerator for up to two*
*weeks.*

TWO *of* CUPS

# The TWO of CUPS

## BASIC DEFINITION

A beautiful card of partnerships, relationships, and new romances, the Two of Cups brings two people together, whether it's through love, work, or friendship. When this card shows up, be prepared to make a soulful connection—a union that is passionate, cooperative, and trusting, and one that will be around for a very long time.

## TEQUILA DEFINITION

A good friend makes you a special drink. They know the exact ingredients you like and have you in mind specifically while making it. This could be a special night out with your significant other: a special toast to you and your love, celebrating the powerful connection you both have for one another. A powerful night of bonding, knowing you found the perfect friend on the perfect night, while sipping the most perfect drink!

## *Reversed* BASIC DEFINITION

Seeing this beautiful card upside down may mean that you simply are not ready to receive love right now. It can also speak of a separation due to disharmony or lack of balance. Sometimes the Two of Cups Reversed means you are blocking your emotions and no one is allowed in right now. It can also mean you have misplaced your affection in the wrong person.

## *Reversed* TEQUILA DEFINITION

A night of drinking has caused you and a good friend to part ways. Maybe you've made a drunken declaration of love and it was not reciprocated. Sometimes we let our emotions get the best of us and things get out of control. Let's just hope you both forget that awkward moment the following morning.

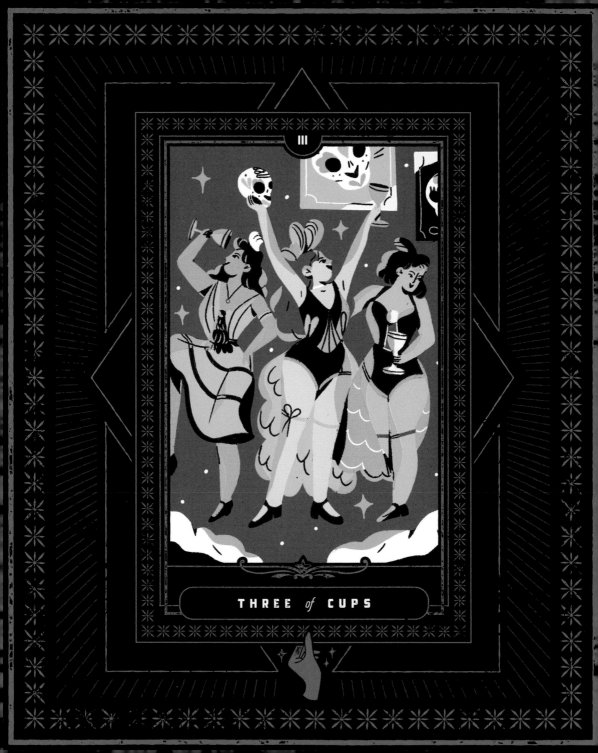

THREE *of* CUPS

# *The* THREE *of* CUPS

## BASIC DEFINITION

Some cards in the tarot are all about having fun, and this is one of them. The Three of Cups validates the good friendships you have in the world. You may even have a fun event arriving in the near future that you'll be able to celebrate together. These are the friends you want! The ones that have your back. In times of trouble and sadness lean on these friends. They'll be fine with it.

## *Reversed* DEFINITION

Sometimes too much of a good thing is just that, too much. The Three of Cups Reversed can refer to a toxic relationship or if you're feeling like you're the third wheel in a relationship. It can also say that your so-called friends have been making you feel left out. Another thing the Three of Cups Reversed asks is, What do you get out of this relationship? Does it bring you joy?

If it doesn't, then why are you still in it?

## TEQUILA DEFINITION

It's Friday night, and it was a particularly long work week. You are super excited to be going out with your people tonight. It's great to know that you have a loyal group of friends who look out for you no matter what. Friends who, if you get a little too drunk and emotional later, will have no problem with that side of you. And you'll never have to apologize to them in the morning.

## *Reversed* TEQUILA DEFINITION

Another night out at the bars with the same group of friends you always seem to hang out with. You enjoy their company, but you feel like the odd person out. They are all talking among themselves about their favorite vodka and you are off to the side, holding your margarita. You know it's time to find a new group of friends, but you also don't want to burn any bridges.

Eventually, it will happen on its own.

THE MINOR ARCANA

# MYSTICAL PAIRING

*A drink for sharing is a drink of caring. Let us use this big-batch cocktail to honor the connections in our lives. The friendship we've had for years to the newest of bonds formed. They all matter, and should all be valued.*

*Use this opportunity to ritualize your relationships with your friends. Within a circle of three, taking turns clockwise, pour from this pitcher of goodness one at a time. Each person should say how they feel about the person to their right. When it comes to your turn to pour, let your friends say something about you. Why do you value each other? Remember times when you were there for each other. What moonlit magic do you make together? Is your bond stronger than gin? What would you do for each other? What would you ask of each other? Toast friendship and drink down heartily!*

*Serve in*     *a wineglass*

# *The*
# THREE OF CUPS COCKTAIL

2 OUNCES LEMON JUICE

1/2 CUCUMBER, SLICED

6 TO 8 RASPBERRIES

1 HANDFUL OF FRESH MINT, TORN

1/2 OUNCE PIMM'S NO. 1

1 OUNCE HENDRICK'S GIN

1 CAN LEMON SODA

1 CAN SELTZER

✦

*Add the juice, fruit, and mint to a 60-ounce pitcher and muddle the fruit. Fill the pitcher with ice. Add the Pimm's and gin and stir with a wooden spoon. Add the lemon soda and seltzer, filling to the top. Stir a couple more times to marry the ingredients. Pour into wineglasses or mason jars.*

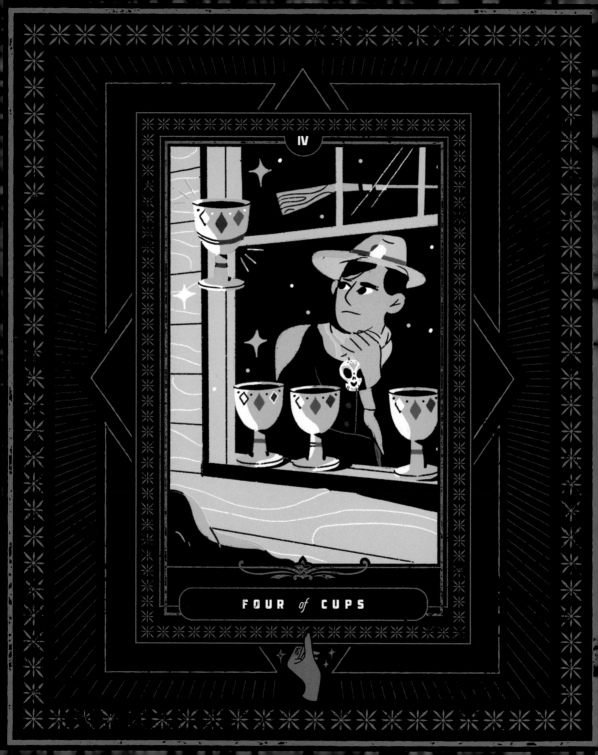

FOUR *of* CUPS

# *The* FOUR *of* CUPS

## BASIC DEFINITION

The Four of Cups reminds us to really look inside ourselves. Do we appreciate all that we have, or are we taking it for granted? The card points out that the grass is not always greener on the other side. It shows that we are wasting valuable time wishing for something that may never come. Why? Because maybe our desires are unrealistic. Take some time out of your busy day to reflect on all that you have and recognize how blessed you truly are.

## TEQUILA DEFINITION

Staring into your añejo, you start questioning your overall happiness. Sometimes when drinking or socializing we get a little apathetic and disillusioned with our place in the world, so we walk off by ourselves and take a time-out to reflect on how we're feeling. Thoughts spin on about imaginary problems and distractions that take us away from being what we should be . . . happy!

## *Reversed* DEFINITION

The Four of Cups Reversed beckons you to take a moment away from feeling pessimistic and to finally appreciate all that you have. Something new might be within your grasp, but you can't see it. You may be too self-absorbed or stubborn to face the fact that you are in a better place than you think you are. Another lesson the Four of Cups Reversed teaches is to stop focusing on all that is lost when you could be discovering how much could be gained instead.

## *Reversed* TEQUILA DEFINITION

You've clearly consumed way more tequila than you should have and are completely missing everything that is going on around you. One of your friends is trying to introduce you to this beauty he knows, but you're too focused on the negative to acknowledge this potential new love connection. Sometimes when you drink you have a tendency to get a little down. Take action and remove yourself from this funk. Possibilities abound—you just have to be able to see them!

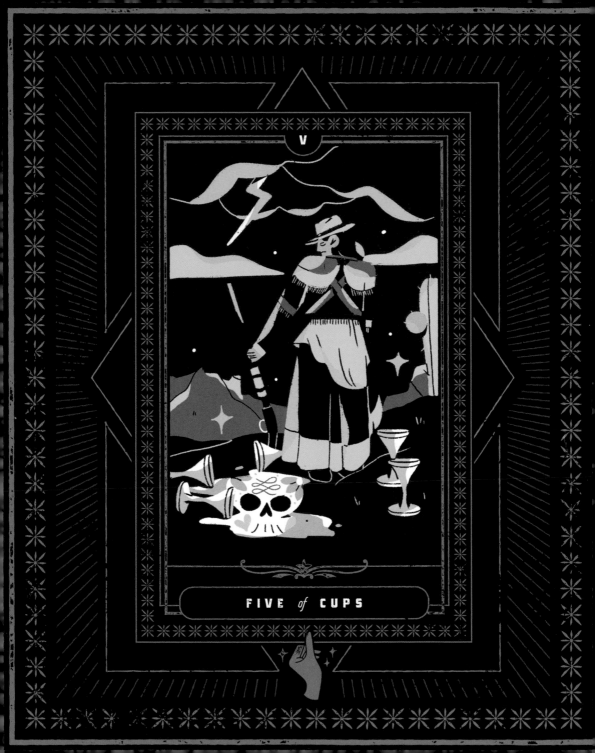

FIVE *of* CUPS

# The FIVE of CUPS

## BASIC DEFINITION

The Five of Cups is aware that you have been through a very trying time. It's possible that a relationship has ended or something has occurred that would cause you feelings of despair and regret. Feelings of isolation and bitterness may be going through your mind, and you're wallowing in the sadness. If you look hard enough, you will still find things in your life that are positives, but they're hard to see. You have to look with a new perspective. Eventually time does heal.

## TEQUILA DEFINITION

While tequila can make some people very happy, other times it can do quite the opposite. The closest of friends can easily have a miscommunication or get into a fight during a night of barhopping and silly escapades. Now what will you do? Are you going to call to apologize or are you going to wait for your friend to make the first move? When you're experiencing the Five of Cups you may not be ready to recover. You may still be stinging from what was said or what was done, the wounds too fresh. What's happened to your friendship is definitely a setback. But try to remain hopeful; this too shall pass.

## *Reversed* DEFINITION

The worst is over with the Five of Cups Reversed, and you can finally look to start on the road to recovery. You've matured emotionally and are hopeful of what the future brings. The trick is letting go and not becoming jaded. There may be a tendency to stay upset instead of letting go of the past problems. But that is something you can control. The two remaining cups that have not spilled over in the image represent the love that remains, and that is sometimes undervalued. Allow the cups to be refilled with light and treasure them.

## *Reversed* TEQUILA DEFINITION

Whatever may have happened the night before needs to be forgiven. Now is not the time to be bitter but is instead the time to show that you can be mature and recover from it. People sometimes get downright mean when they've had too much to drink. They say things that are not easily forgotten. Let's keep that in the back of our minds before we let things become irreparable. I'm sure in a week or two, you'll be toasting with whomever you had the drama.

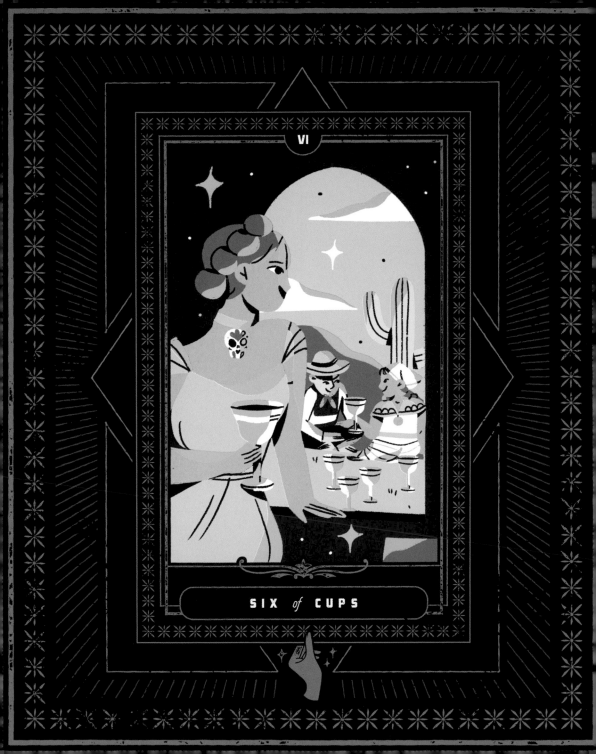

# *The* SIX *of* CUPS

## BASIC DEFINITION

This loving card shows happy memories. What's happened in your life to make you feel so nostalgic? Has someone from the past whom you were very close to shown up and have you been thinking about a time of innocence, simple pleasures, and youth? You may be able to find temporary joy from this feeling, but it isn't smart to spend too much time thinking about the past when we have the "right now," which is so much more important. This card can also represent someone offering gratitude or an apology that you've been patiently waiting to hear.

## *Reversed* BASIC DEFINITION

While the Six of Cups talks about reconnecting with your past, the Six of Cups Reversed warns of being stuck there. This card can mean that you regret past actions and are obsessing over mistakes you have made. We all know that person who won't let go of the leather jacket they've been wearing since 1995, right? It's also sad when that friend of yours can't recover from a past breakup because they never received the closure they were looking for. The Six of Cups Reversed can keep us from moving forward if we let it.

## TEQUILA DEFINITION

The Six of Cups can represent a high school or college reunion where you will share a drink with old friends and reconnect. Maybe you're single now and that person you used to pine over is single, too. Will you capitalize on this celebration that has brought the two of you together again? Toasting your tequilas really drives this event home, and for a second or two, you are back in college feeling the same feelings you felt when you were twenty-one.

## *Reversed* TEQUILA DEFINITION

The underaged kid trying to get into the bar with a fake ID could be a reversed Six of Cups moment. Spending your whole life in the college town where you went to school shows you could be afraid to move on with your life. Maybe you can't leave until you and an old friend make amends. What makes the perfect apology gift? Glad you asked—tequila, of course!

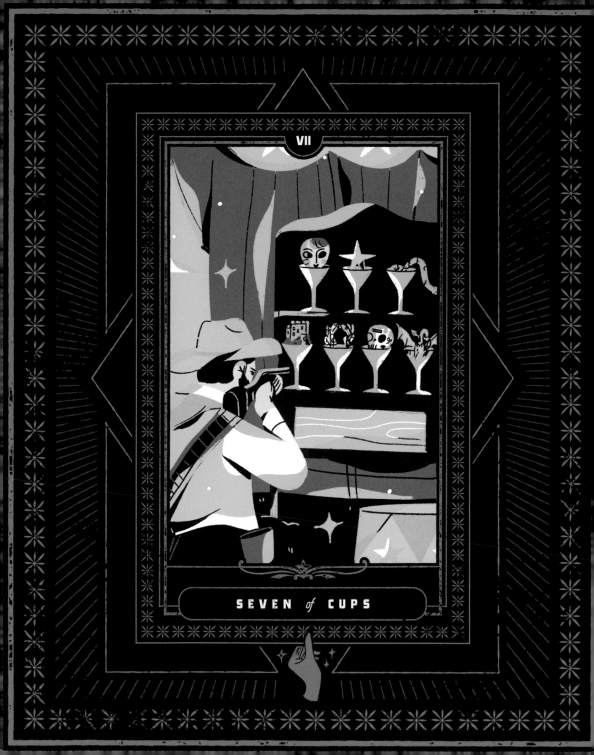

# The SEVEN of CUPS

## BASIC DEFINITION

This is the card of indecision. It's good to have choices available to you. However, the Seven of Cups warns that having too many choices can leave you feeling indecisive. That's because you just aren't ready to make any decisions based on the information you currently have available. There is a tendency to fantasize about all your options. It's also easy to allow yourself to get lost in the illusion of possibilities and end up choosing nothing. If you are faced with a tough decision, then don't rush it, of course. But if you are choosing what you want to eat off the menu, just decide. Is it really worth all the debate?

## Reversed BASIC DEFINITION

The days of indecision are behind you. You've been at a standstill for a long time now and you finally have the determination and strong will to make a definitive decision. The Seven of Cups Reversed can also refer to avoiding a decision that you know you have to make. You keep putting it off in hopes that it will just resolve itself. Sometimes you're so overwhelmed with indecision that you make a choice out of desperation and necessity.

## TEQUILA DEFINITION

This is by far the best tequila bar you've ever been to. The tacos are delicious and the small plates have been a hit. You've just had a spicy margarita but are now trying to decide what your next drink should be. The menu has twenty-plus options, and they all look equally delicious. You clearly can't try them all tonight. So how are you going to make up your mind? Remember it's only a cocktail menu; it's not going to alter your life for good. Do yourself and your impatient friends a favor and just pick something.

## Reversed TEQUILA DEFINITION

In the days of wine and roses we have so many choices. Going from place to place, drink in hand, meeting so many people. How does one settle on a person to open their heart to? It took you an hour to choose the right attire for the night, and how long did you spend annoying the bartender with your questions about the cocktail menu? Make sure you aren't wasting your time on the decisions that don't really matter. Don't use indecision as a form of fantasy or escapism. If you're not sure what you want, just follow your true self and listen. The answer is most likely right there in front of you.

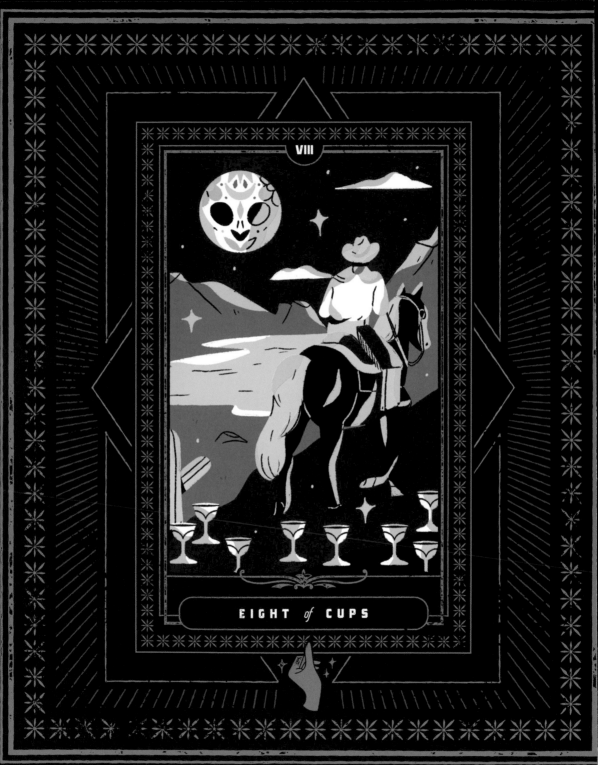

# The EIGHT of CUPS

## BASIC DEFINITION

The Eight of Cups is all about walking away. You've come to a point in your life where you are looking for a deeper and more spiritual purpose. Letting the past go is not an easy thing. You've built up an emotional wall you now want to knock down or, at the very least, walk away from. The Eight of Cups says you can achieve what you want. Don't worry about disappointing those you are abandoning. They've likely seen the change inside you and knew it was coming. All that's left for you to do is embrace the unknown and go live your new best life.

## Reversed BASIC DEFINITION

Just like the Eight of Cups talks about letting go and walking away from a situation that holds nothing good for you anymore, the Eight of Cups Reversed refers to being uncertain about letting go of your past and moving on. You want to leave, but you can't. There is something (or perhaps several things) keeping you here and yet you know they no longer serve you any purpose. You're feeling stuck and are questioning your plan to follow your true self.

## TEQUILA DEFINITION

Are you able to stop the tequila lifestyle you've been living for some time now? A friend asked you to join them on a cleanse to jump-start an intense diet, and you know deep down it is exactly what you need. You don't want to turn your back on your social circle, but you need something more from your life right now—more than just socializing and material desires. Say hello to the wonderful world of juicing and veggies.

## Reversed TEQUILA DEFINITION

You've decided to move away from the people and things that no longer have your best interests in mind. You've packed your bags and relocated far enough away so you can start over. But for some reason, you're beginning to regret the choice of leaving the life you've had for the past decade. Now you're uncertain and more miserable than you were before you left. You have to be able to follow your dreams and release the fear that is blocking your momentum. Maybe you need to take some time looking inward before you can truly be happy with your new home and starting over. Just know that this move is for the best and that you should have faith in the decision you've made.

# _The_ MYSTICAL PAIRING

_It's very hard to abandon things you've once held dear. Maybe it's a relationship that has turned sour or a job that no longer sparks joy. It's possible you are on the verge of a spiritual awakening and you have to let go of old beliefs that no longer serve._

_One night after a particularly trying day, let your ritual of transition take hold. Once the cocktail is prepared, open your front door and step outside. While standing on your steps or porch, take a sip of the rich bourbon and bitters. Let the flavors swirl in your mouth, crashing against your taste buds like waves on a beach. Let this be the first step in many to embracing your new life's adventure. Look up to the moon and raise your glass high. Cheers to yourself! Cheers to the moon! And most of all, cheers to all of the people holding you back and keeping you down that you will never see again!_

_Serve in_     _a double rocks glass_

# The
# EIGHT OF CUPS COCKTAIL

3 OUNCES PENELOPE BOURBON

4 DASHES ANGOSTURA BITTERS

1 OUNCE BROWN BUTTER SYRUP [RECIPE FOLLOWS]

ORANGE PEEL, FOR GARNISH [FLAME OPTIONAL; SEE PAGE 9]

✦

*Add all the ingredients to a mixing glass and stir 12 times each way until condensation occurs. Strain into a double rocks glass with a large ice block or cube. Mist the orange peel oils over the drink.*

### BROWN BUTTER SYRUP

*Put 1 cup water, 1 cup coconut sugar, 1 teaspoon cinnamon, 6 drops butter extract, and a pinch of salt into a saucepan. Cook over medium heat, stirring, until the sugar is dissolved. Chill overnight and keep in the refrigerator for up to two weeks.*

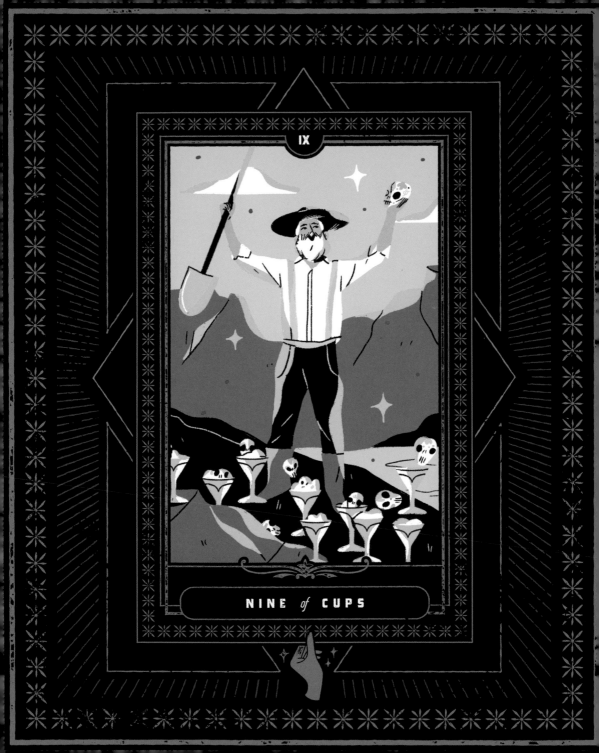

# The NINE of CUPS

## BASIC DEFINITION

The Nine of Cups is letting you know that the universe is preparing a gift in your name. If you were to make a wish, what would it be? Because when this card shows up, your dreams may just come true. It indicates a time of pleasures, contentment, and success, so embrace it. Will you allow yourself to accept the gifts that have been provided? Are you able to show the gratitude necessary to continue your forward momentum to your higher self?

## TEQUILA DEFINITION

You sure are living your best life. You can afford to buy the best tequilas, and you enjoy sitting at your bar and just staring at them. It's not a problem. It's just that you are happy with your collection and you like spending time appreciating it. You aren't even a big drinker. You just prefer tequila and when you drink it, you want the best.

## Reversed BASIC DEFINITION

The Nine of Cups Reversed is still a positive card except for a couple of differences. When you have everything you desire, that doesn't mean you're happy. Is materialism the answer to your happiness? Maybe overindulgence is? Have your tastes and happiness become so grandiose that you can no longer find joy in the simple things? Will your desires ever truly be satiated? Try to remain a happy, giving person now that you are at a place where you can truly make a difference.

## Reversed TEQUILA DEFINITION

Don't get me wrong—your friends still like hanging out with you. However, your expensive tastes can make it hard for them to keep up with you. You may have no problem picking up the tab, but your friends may have an issue with it. At the end of the night, your best friend pulls you aside and lets you know that you have, in fact, changed and that your gift of newfound luck, money, and happiness may also have its drawbacks. Your friend reassures you that they all still love you, but seriously, just quit the excess and materialistic tendencies, okay? It's just not necessary.

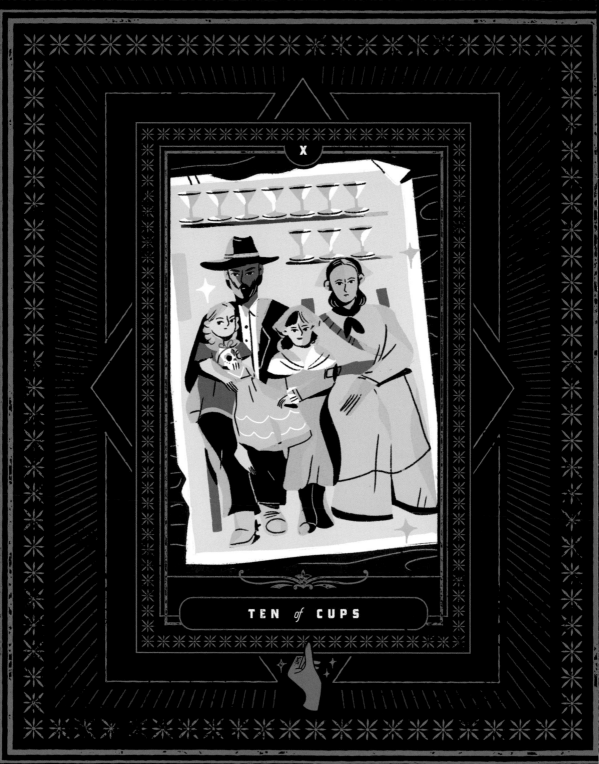

TEN *of* CUPS

# *The* TEN *of* CUPS

## BASIC DEFINITION

The Ten of Cups is always a welcome card in a reading. It is the full expression and manifestation of all of the Cups cards. It speaks to finding your soul mate, full love, strong connections, and a happy marriage. If you have a question about your family and this card shows up, consider it a very good sign. You have the romantic fulfillment you've been looking for, and you can consider yourself very blessed that you have such a supportive and loving circle of friends and family.

## TEQUILA DEFINITION

On the day of your wedding anniversary, the two of you decide to go to a cute little bed-and-breakfast to celebrate the true love you share for each other. A shared toast in your firelit room after a romantic dinner is the best anniversary you could have asked for. When you get back home from the weekend, your parents and your kids throw you a surprise party because they, too, want to share in the blessed event. Your whole family shows you their love, and at that very moment you know the feeling of the Ten of Cups.

## *Reversed* BASIC DEFINITION

The Ten of Cups Reversed reminds us that even in the strongest of families there will still be times of friction and disharmony. This card may point to separations and divorce if surrounded by other negative cards. If you receive the Ten of Cups Reversed in a reading, though, don't expect the worst. Just remember that most problems stem from miscommunication and unrealistic expectations we have for one another. Any problem that you're facing, the Ten of Cups Reversed still reminds you that the love you have in your life is stronger than any problems that may be happening at this present time.

## *Reversed* TEQUILA DEFINITION

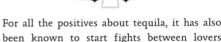

For all the positives about tequila, it has also been known to start fights between lovers and friends. Drinking can equal problematic communicating that can lead to grief. Mostly they're harmless misunderstandings. But they also can get a little out of hand if you let them persist without any reconciliation. Never fear, though: the love of the Ten of Cups, reversed or not, is a big love that can always endure.

# The
# MYSTICAL PAIRING

*Embrace your senses with the Ten of Cups cocktail. The number ten in the tarot represents completion. Celebrate the ending or beginning of a new cycle with this positively empowering beverage.*

*Friends can be family, and of course family can be friends. They're interchangeable if the love is there. How would you celebrate a complete and all-encompassing love?*

*Let's start with this recipe. Ingredients like rose water, CBD oil, and a sweet, refreshing ale are a wonderful place to start. On a night when your loved ones are together, prepare this cocktail and grab a lot of straws. Sharing is an important part of this ritual, and you wouldn't want to miss out.*

*Have everyone involved sit at a table and place a straw for each into the drink. Place white and gold candles in the center of the table, each candle representing a specific family member. Moving in a clockwise pattern, pass the cocktail as you say a positive affirmation about your family and those around you before taking a sip from your selected straw. Remember to stay focused and positive throughout this ritual. If you sense any negativity, please start over. Make a couple, just in case.*

*Serve in*     *a collins glass*

# *The*
# TEN OF CUPS COCKTAIL

1 1/2 OUNCES TITO'S HANDMADE VODKA

1/2 OUNCE LIME JUICE

1/4 OUNCE ROSE WATER

3 OUNCES LINDEMANS FRAMBOISE

1 DROP CBD OIL FOR TWO PEOPLE, 2 DROPS FOR FOUR

ROSE PETAL, FOR GARNISH

*Place the vodka, lime juice, and rose water in a cocktail shaker. Cover and shake. Strain into a collins glass with ice. Add the framboise and garnish with a rose petal. This drink should be shared and passed among friends. Each friend should have their own straw.*

PAGE *of* CUPS

# The PAGE of CUPS

## BASIC DEFINITION

The Page of Cups brings the message of an open and joyful heart. A love letter would be the perfect example of this card. The Page of Cups can also represent a new development or a new creative start. This card may indicate that new love is right around the corner, a love that makes you feel like you're a teenager again, a dreamy love. At times it can also refer to a new birth or pregnancy.

## TEQUILA DEFINITION

You've just opened up a brand-new restaurant and are excited for your opening night! You've sent out a bunch of special invitations to your closest friends, family, and investors and are beaming with excitement. This new venture has been in development for quite some time now, and anyone receiving their special invite in the mail knows how important this is for you. It's the beginning of something beautiful and creative, and maybe, just maybe, it'll be the first of many more to come.

## Reversed BASIC DEFINITION

We all let our emotions get the best of us, and if the Page of Cups Reversed shows up in a tarot reading, chances are your view of love may be a bit immature. Love is a process, and you have to crawl before you can walk. Feelings of emotional instability and being overly sensitive are signs that your love needs to mature. If this card shows up in a reading that is not about love, I would say that you're being creatively blocked and cannot show the world what you are truly capable of, at least not right now.

## Reversed TEQUILA DEFINITION

It's late, and it's safe to say you've probably had a bit too much to drink. Listening to some overly emotional music has you feeling lonely. So you pick up your phone and start drunk texting an ex-love of yours. Continuing with your overly dramatic and seductive messages, you hope that for the rest of the night you will be preoccupied. Knowing that this is not the answer, you hope it's at least the answer right now.

KNIGHT *of* CUPS

# The KNIGHT of CUPS

## BASIC DEFINITION

The Knight of Cups embodies the hopeless romantic. This person is a dreamer, and they are very passionate about seeking that true connection. When this card shows up in a tarot reading, love can be on the way. Romance and chivalry are not dead when it comes to the Knight of Cups. Still, having a tendency to be immature, the Knight of Cups may wear their hearts on their sleeves. When this card speaks about your relationship, assume it's very passionate; however, realize that true love endures. It doesn't just get set ablaze and burn away.

## *Reversed* BASIC DEFINITION

Love makes us do silly things. It can also make us moody, jealous, and selfish. When the Knight of Cups shows up reversed it can mean that you are not open to love right now. This is not the right time for you to be entering into a new relationship because you're still feeling a bit jaded and emotionally unavailable from how your last relationship ended. You can't force how you feel about someone, so it's better to put off any new relationships until the wounds of the past have healed.

## TEQUILA DEFINITION

You see that person at the end of the bar? The one who smiles at you from time to time? They just bought you a drink and asked if they can sit down next to you. Now, making an origami bird from a bar napkin, they hand it over to you, smiling with sincerity. There is something so nice about this romantic pickup approach. You can't help but wonder if this is something this person does often. The approach is a little too perfect.

## *Reversed* TEQUILA DEFINITION

Some people you can see coming from a mile away. The person who's trying too hard, a player, someone who has the word "trickery" written all over them is buzzing all about the dance floor. Flirting with different people, they may come across a bit like a drunken butterfly. Completely unreliable and, even though they seem to be genuinely interested in getting to know you, they really aren't open to love at all. Hopefully you won't end up another in a long line of one-KNIGHT stands.

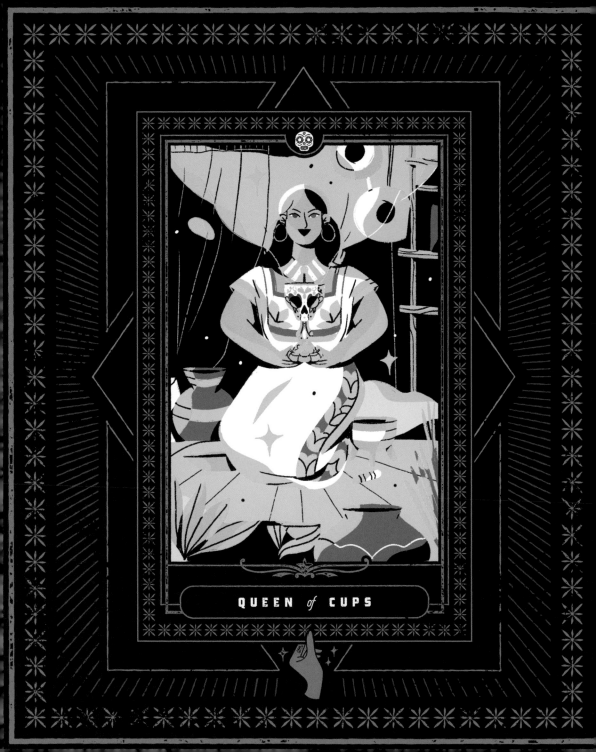

QUEEN *of* CUPS

# The QUEEN of CUPS

## BASIC DEFINITION

The Queen of Cups is an emotionally together individual: very strong and sensitive, often leading with the heart. However, they are wiser than they may appear. They have a strong intuitive side, often making it easy to see who a person is on the inside. When the Queen shows up in a tarot reading, be aware of your emotions. Allow yourself to be led with a trusting heart and have faith that you are making the right decisions.

## *Reversed* BASIC DEFINITION

This reversed Queen can let their emotions get carried away. They embody the aspects of love that can be very unhealthy and even lead to alcohol or substance abuse. Words like dependent, delusion, depravity, and insensitivity can paint a distressing picture of the Queen of Cups Reversed. However, just because you are feeling like this right now doesn't mean that you will stay this way forever. You just need to work through the pain you haven't been able to let go of, and then, eventually, you will be able to embrace some of the wonderful aspects of love.

## TEQUILA DEFINITION

Just the thought of getting back into the dating scene would have made you nauseous a year ago, but surprisingly you're becoming quite the natural at it. You are able to juggle your nurturing mother side, as well as find the time to go on a date from time to time. But you'll only go on dates that you have a good feeling about. You have enough wisdom to know not to rush into anything serious right away, especially having two small children at home. You are an expert at love—you're just not foolish about it.

## *Reversed* TEQUILA DEFINITION

The Queen of Cups Reversed is overly emotional and out to make a scene. See the person throwing a fit on the dance floor? The one yelling over the music at some poor person who, unfortunately, said the wrong thing at the wrong time? The reversed Queen can be a bit volatile, especially when drinking and feeling insecure. What this Queen needs is their carriage to take them home before they completely turn into a pumpkin.

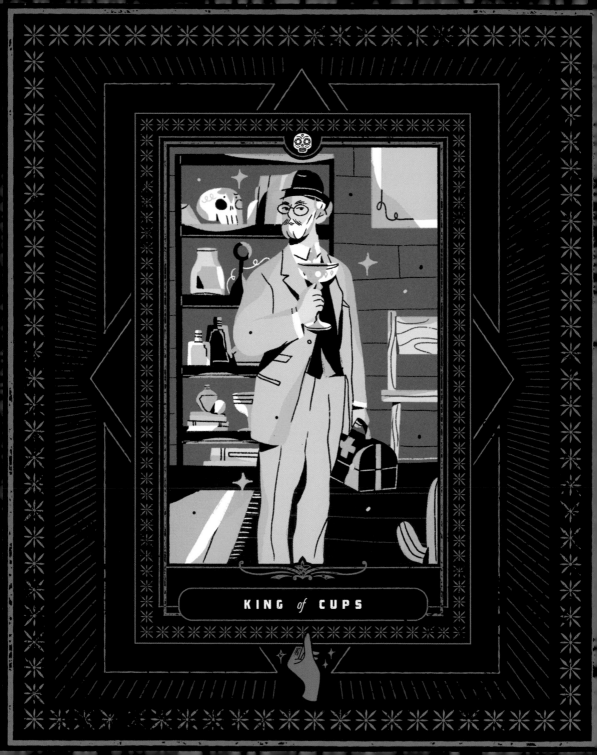

KING *of* CUPS

# The KING of CUPS

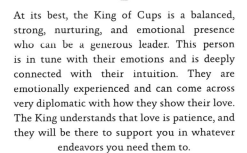

## BASIC DEFINITION

At its best, the King of Cups is a balanced, strong, nurturing, and emotional presence who can be a generous leader. This person is in tune with their emotions and is deeply connected with their intuition. They are emotionally experienced and can come across very diplomatic with how they show their love. The King understands that love is patience, and they will be there to support you in whatever endeavors you need them to.

## *Reversed* BASIC DEFINITION

Some people can't get a grip on their emotions and let them consume them. The King of Cups Reversed can be moody and even have an explosive temper. They can also be overly sentimental and a pushover. Either way, neither is optimal. Sometimes the King of Cups can abuse their leadership role by being manipulative. On the positive side, the reversed King can choose to look inward and take this opportunity to achieve some much-needed self-care.

## TEQUILA DEFINITION

There are many people who at times embody the King of Cups: anyone who helps their friends consistently with life issues, the person who puts up with all the drunken confessions and offers sage advice that may actually be considered because it's that good. They may as well be a substance abuse counselor, because they have all the attributes of a strong, supportive, kind, and compassionate listener and healer.

## *Reversed* TEQUILA DEFINITION

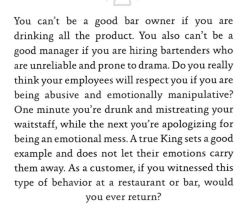

You can't be a good bar owner if you are drinking all the product. You also can't be a good manager if you are hiring bartenders who are unreliable and prone to drama. Do you really think your employees will respect you if you are being abusive and emotionally manipulative? One minute you're drunk and mistreating your waitstaff, while the next you're apologizing for being an emotional mess. A true King sets a good example and does not let their emotions carry them away. As a customer, if you witnessed this type of behavior at a restaurant or bar, would you ever return?

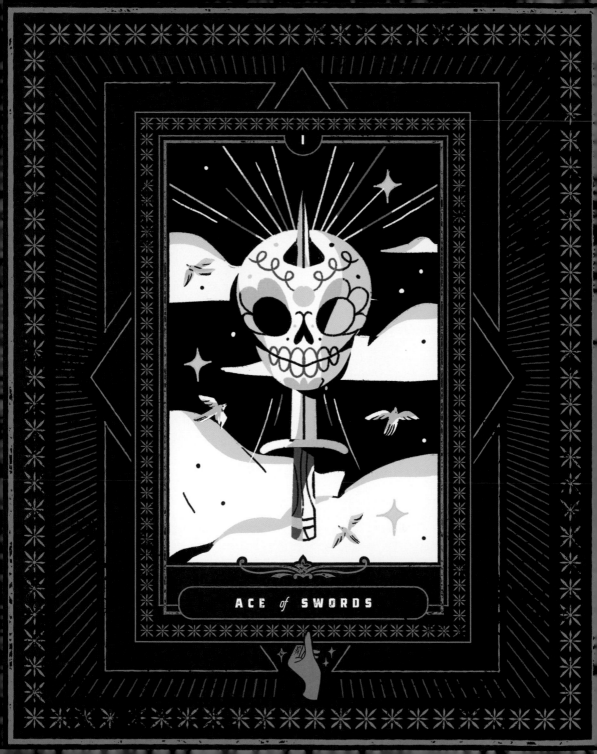

ACE *of* SWORDS

# *The* ACE *of* SWORDS

✳✳✳✳✳✳✳✳✳✳✳✳✳✳✳✳✳✳✳✳✳✳✳✳✳✳✳✳✳✳✳✳

## BASIC DEFINITION

Aces are beginnings. And the Ace of Swords is saying that you're on the verge of a breakthrough. You've received that "aha" moment from the universe and your goals and desires are being seen with a refreshing, new mental clarity. Maybe you've just figured out what you want to do with your life and you want to tell all your family and friends about this realized truth. Swords can speak to communication, so it's possible you are considering a new career, one in which you are in the position to speak your truth and be very successful at it.

## *Reversed* BASIC DEFINITION

How are you able to move forward when you can't see clearly what it is that you want? When confusion and scattered thoughts are flying through your brain, you might be feeling some Ace of Swords Reversed energy. When inspiration has to be put off because it's not completely realized, that's fine; don't rush it. Your breakthrough will happen when it's time. It's frustrating to know you have an idea you want to share with the world, but it's just not fully developed yet. Your big moment is almost here, but you don't want to make any poor decisions, so just sit on it, and the breakthrough will come shortly.

## TEQUILA DEFINITION

Culinary school was the best decision you ever made. You've known that you have wanted to be a chef your whole life. Graduating with your degree was the happiest day of your life, and getting that first job in the restaurant of your dreams was unbelievable. It's a great feeling when you know in your bones what you want to do with your life, and you set out to do it. Nothing or no one can stop you. Your next breakthrough, you know, will be starting your own restaurant! You can taste the success on your tongue; it's only a matter of time.

## *Reversed* TEQUILA DEFINITION

It's your sophomore year in college and you want to change your major. You thought you knew exactly what you wanted to do with your life, but for some reason the perception you've had about this particular major is not working out. It's possible that you're overanalyzing. You may be worried that your parents won't understand your reconsideration, but you know you have to follow your desire. This isn't the beginning that you initially were hoping for, but it's still a beginning. Once you get through the obstacles presented, you'll acclimate just fine.

# The
# MYSTICAL PAIRING

*In a world with so many people and so much communication, how can we filter through to the universal truths? How can we block out the scams and the lies? How do we know who to trust?*

*When the world has thrown you a curveball and you need to think through your situation with a clear focused intent then this is the drink for you. Grab a Hemingway book and boldly read aloud a paragraph that captures his adventurous spirit. You will need to tap into that type of energy to break through all the daily garbage to find the hidden gems.*

*When shaking the ingredients of this cocktail, do not allow yourself to get all emotional. You need a clear, logical mind to overcome those pesky feelings that so often get in the way of making the right choice. Let the honest flavors of the Ace of Swords guide you to victory and a new beginning!*

*Serve in* a champagne glass

# *The* ACE OF SWORDS COCKTAIL

2 OUNCES PAPA PILAR RUM INFUSED WITH JALAPEÑO

1 OUNCE ORANGE JUICE

1 OUNCE CARROT JUICE

1 OUNCE LIME JUICE

1/2 OUNCE HONEY SIMPLE SYRUP [SEE PAGE 43]

1/2 OUNCE GARBANZO BEAN WATER

1 FRESH SPRIG OF DILL, FOR GARNISH

✦

*Add all the ingredients into a cocktail shaker. Cover and vigorously shake. Really let loose. Strain into a champagne glass and garnish with a spanked sprig of dill—clap the dill with both hands to bring out the aromatics.*

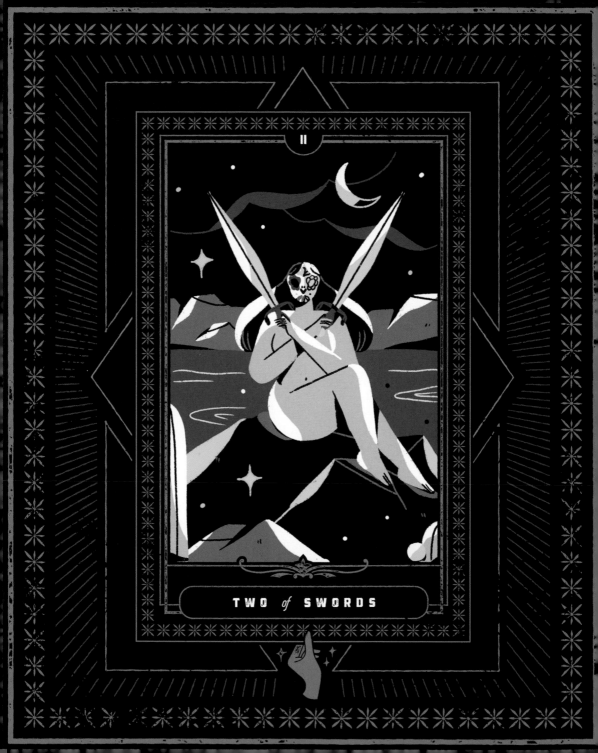

TWO *of* SWORDS

# The TWO of SWORDS

## BASIC DEFINITION

The Two of Swords talks about the inability to make a decision with the information you are presented with. It can feel like a stalemate. Some choices that you are given are so bad that your best choice is to make no choice at all. You decide to look inward. The impasse you are facing is just too unsettling. So instead of making a decision you'll probably later regret, you choose to remain still. You'll be able to put the decision off for a while, or maybe you have already been doing that. However, the time will come when you will have to pull the trigger and make a decision. You can't hold out forever.

## Reversed BASIC DEFINITION

The "between a rock and a hard place" card. For whatever reason, you're being faced with a decision that has no positive outcome. Trying to find the better of two evils, you are completely stuck with inactivity. Whatever you decide will have repercussions that are unavoidable. Have faith and trust your instincts. All there is left to do is hope you've made the right choice.

## TEQUILA DEFINITION

It's tough having two best friends. It's also tough being stuck in the middle of those two friends. One likes this bar, the other likes that bar. And honestly, you don't really care where you go. The problem is you don't like picking sides, and you hate that you are being forced to choose between the two. Even in a situation as mundane as this, why should your decision be the winning vote? You've done it before and you'll probably do it again, but tonight you're saying to hell with it, and just staying in.

## Reversed TEQUILA DEFINITION

Drinking can often lead to arguments and saying things we don't mean to those we love. Emotional ultimatums are sometimes given that we would never convey when sober. If you can push off saying the things that you know will get you into trouble until the following morning, it'll save you from having a big problem tonight. Silence can be its own big statement, and it also keeps you from sticking your foot in your mouth.

# The
# MYSTICAL PAIRING

*The Two of Swords is a card of decision-making, or should I say the inability to make a decision. No one likes the uncomfortable feeling of indecisiveness, so use this recipe to remove your mental block.*

*Take in the aroma of ginger and let it elevate you. Allow the clear blanco tequila to be overcome by colors just as your mind will be overcome with ideas. Muddle the blueberries and imagine how the clouds in your mind will be swept away as if by a broom.*

*Light two white candles and grab a pencil and paper to make a list. Record all the pros and cons that accompany the decision you are having a problem with. Meditate on your answers and then light your list ablaze with the candles. Also try imagining another person seated across from you. Practice giving them advice about the same situation you are having trouble with. It's always easier to help others than it is to help yourself.*

*Serve in*   *a collins glass*

# *The*
# TWO OF SWORDS COCKTAIL

6 TO 8 BLUEBERRIES, PLUS MORE FOR GARNISH

1 1/2 OUNCES LEMON JUICE

1 1/2 OUNCES BLANCO TEQUILA

1/2 OUNCE DOMAINE DE CANTON

1/2 OUNCE MAPLE SYRUP

✦

*In a cocktail shaker without ice, muddle the blueberries and lemon juice. Add ice and all the remaining ingredients. Shake vigorously until condensation occurs on the outside of the shaker. Strain into a collins glass with ice. Garnish with a stick of blueberries.*

THREE *of* SWORDS

# The THREE of SWORDS

## BASIC DEFINITION

The breakup card. The Three of Swords is another card that no one really likes to see show up in a reading. The main definitions include betrayal, heartbreak, and loss. At first glance, most people think the breakup refers to their love life; however, that may not necessarily be true. It can indicate a falling-out with friends or family or maybe a lost business relationship. This card usually brings rejection and pain, but it can also bring personal growth if you allow yourself to see it.

## *Reversed* BASIC DEFINITION

The pain from the Three of Swords is over and now you can start to heal. Sometimes the reversal of this card can mean you are unable to move on, but that's mostly in extreme cases. For the most part, the Three of Swords Reversed refers to forgiveness and releasing the pain you've been holding on to for some time. At times this card can also ask the hard question of whether or not you are needlessly cutting people out of your life. It's possible that you're confused, overly suspicious, or overthinking, to the point where you just want to leave and be by yourself.

## TEQUILA DEFINITION

No one likes breaking up over the phone, but having it happen when you're out socially is no picnic either. Regardless, it was just done, and a million emotions are rushing through your body. You reach for your drink and try your best to look unaffected; however, inside you're devastated. You excuse yourself from the awkwardness and find a place where you can collect yourself. You may not realize it now, but you'll find a new love very soon, one that will make you forget all about what just happened.

## *Reversed* TEQUILA DEFINITION

People drink for many reasons. Some choose to go out and have fun, while there are others who turn to tequila for answers when they are upset or going through a hard time. It's difficult being stuck in grief or despair and not wanting to talk to anyone about what's going on. You've decided to heal on your own, but is this isolating behavior actually helping you? Instead of drinking to avoid interactions you'd rather not have, talk to someone you trust about what you're going through. It will help you heal.

FOUR *of* SWORDS

# The FOUR of SWORDS

## BASIC DEFINITION

The Four of Swords reminds you to take a much-needed time-out. You have been running on fumes lately. Recovering from the painful Three of Swords, you desperately need to return to your center. The body and mind need time to heal from the burnout and you may need to rediscover self-love. There's nothing wrong with taking some "me time" to recuperate and recharge. Take a weekend of sleeping in and massages. That sounds like a great couple of days to me.

## TEQUILA DEFINITION

Returning from your Vegas holiday, you honestly don't even feel like you've been on a break. Is it possible you need a vacation from your vacation? How can you possibly go back to work feeling this drained? Five days of nonstop partying is getting harder and harder to do with each passing year. This time, you'll take a couple extra days to rest. Turn off your phone and just sleep. Sleep to let your body recover and recharge.

## Reversed BASIC DEFINITION

Where the Four of Swords speaks to rest and recuperation, the Four of Swords Reversed represents not being able to. You need to focus your energy on yourself right now. Keeping up this stressful work schedule is exhausting. You've seen what stress can do to people, and you are worried the same thing will happen to you. Do yourself a favor and schedule some "me time."

## Reversed TEQUILA DEFINITION

Your night started at 8:30 p.m. when you met a couple of friends at the local town bar. You've spent an hour here, and already your friends start getting antsy and want to leave. It's now 10:00 p.m. and your friends look like they're just getting started. After hopping to another two bars it's now 1:00 a.m. and you're toast. Yawn after yawn and worried that your friends will see you slipping into a waking dream state, you excuse yourself and go home.

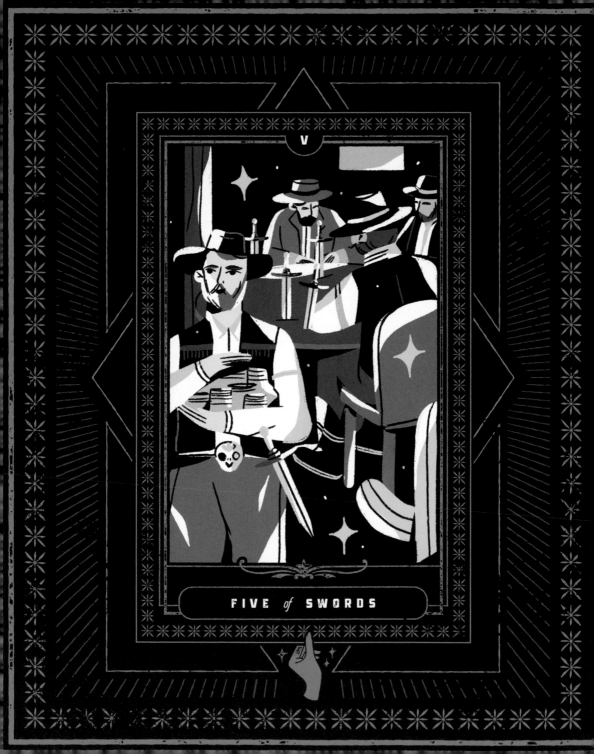

FIVE *of* SWORDS

# The FIVE of SWORDS

✳✳✳✳✳✳✳✳✳✳✳✳✳✳✳✳✳✳✳✳✳✳✳✳✳✳✳✳✳✳✳✳✳✳✳✳

## BASIC DEFINITION

This card defines conflict. The Five of Swords depicts all the problems that can occur through poor communication. Some perfect examples include bullying, manipulation, and making someone feel bad so you can feel better. Dishonorable behavior and winning at all costs show the nasty side of the Five of Swords. However, there is always a chance to learn from the tarot, and the takeaway from this card is to remember to be cognizant of how you communicate and treat those around you.

## *Reversed* BASIC DEFINITION

It's time to forgive and forget. While conflict is getting underway with the Five of Swords, the reversed meaning of this card represents peace. It's not easy to make amends, but it's a part of our overall spiritual growth. Just think how easy it is to make someone feel small. It's a lot harder to offer up an apology and take it back. The Five of Swords Reversed can also represent past actions that have led you to feel dejected and now suspicious of how future interactions will be handled with those who had mistreated you. You may be feeling resentful and not willing to let go. That's the unfortunate flip side of the Five of Swords Reversed.

## TEQUILA DEFINITION

Why do some people bully others? It starts in school and continues as we become adults. Drinking lowers your inhibitions, makes things too easy to say sometimes. What is it we gain from making someone feel bad so we can feel better? The next time you've had one too many, consider the words before you say them. Don't profit at someone else's expense.

## *Reversed* TEQUILA DEFINITION

Remember that fight you and your significant other had last night? The one where you'd love to blame the tequila for all that was said but you know you can't? You know that it was mostly your fault, but you want to forgive and forget that unpleasantness and move past it. You hope the desire for peace will outweigh the desire to stay angry. Maybe a forgiveness toast will help with the healing process.

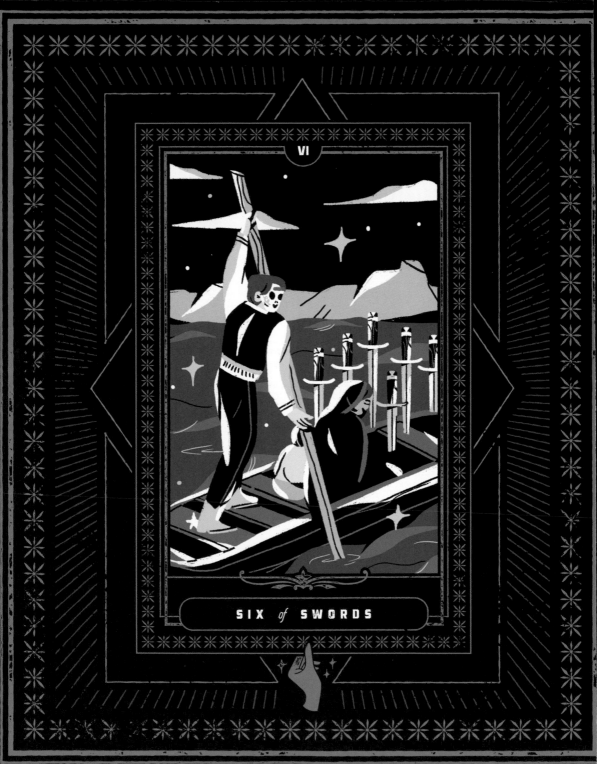

# The SIX of SWORDS

✳✳✳✳✳✳✳✳✳✳✳✳✳✳✳✳✳✳✳✳✳✳✳✳✳✳✳✳✳✳✳✳✳✳✳✳✳

## BASIC DEFINITION

The Six of Swords invites you to take a journey toward both physical and spiritual harmony. You are moving toward smoother waters! Allow yourself to let go of the past and all the drama that came along with it.

## *Reversed* BASIC DEFINITION

In reverse, this card speaks about plans being canceled. It forewarns difficulties about letting go of the past and being unable to move forward. Maybe you had to postpone your island getaway because you got stuck with too much work? The Six of Swords Reversed asks you to question if your planned move is one you should be taking.

## TEQUILA DEFINITION

Take a booze cruise! The weeks are becoming monotonous, and a much-needed break will do you some good. A planned night out with allotted time for margaritas is in your future. Consider calling an Uber for the night so you don't have to worry about an unsavory outcome.

## *Reversed* TEQUILA DEFINITION

Plans get canceled. You had a wonderful night of tequila and tacos planned with your friends, but unfortunately it fell through. Drinking your problems away so you can escape might not be the best decision.

# The
# MYSTICAL PAIRING

*Can you smell the sweet, peppery fragrance? Is it calling you from somewhere far away? A place familiar in your dreams? Or unknown on a continent far away? Is it calling you to find new beginnings? Think about why you need your new start and where you will be making it. There is the excitement of leaving the old you behind combined with the growth and personal achievement awaiting you. Don't carry your familiarities with you! While on your travels across the sea or through the stars, embrace the new flavors flitting around your senses. As you sip this rite of passage, understand the need for change and acknowledge that what's holding you back from your full potential is only yourself.*

*Serve in* a rocks glass

# *The* SIX OF SWORDS COCKTAIL

2 OUNCES BLANCO TEQUILA

1 OUNCE BLACKBERRY PUREE

1 OUNCE LIME JUICE

1 OUNCE BLACK PEPPERCORN SYRUP [RECIPE FOLLOWS]

SEA SALT AND SUGAR, FOR RIM

✦

*Add ice to a cocktail shaker. Add all of the ingredients and shake well. Place some salt and sugar on a plate. Press the rim of a chilled 12-ounce glass into the mixture to coat the edge. Strain the drink into the glass over fresh ice.*

### BLACK PEPPERCORN SYRUP

*Put 2 tablespoons whole black peppercorns, 1 cup water, and 1 cup sugar into a saucepan. Cook over medium heat until the sugar is dissolved. Reduce the heat and simmer for 15 minutes. Discard the peppercorns and chill the syrup overnight. This keeps for two weeks, refrigerated.*

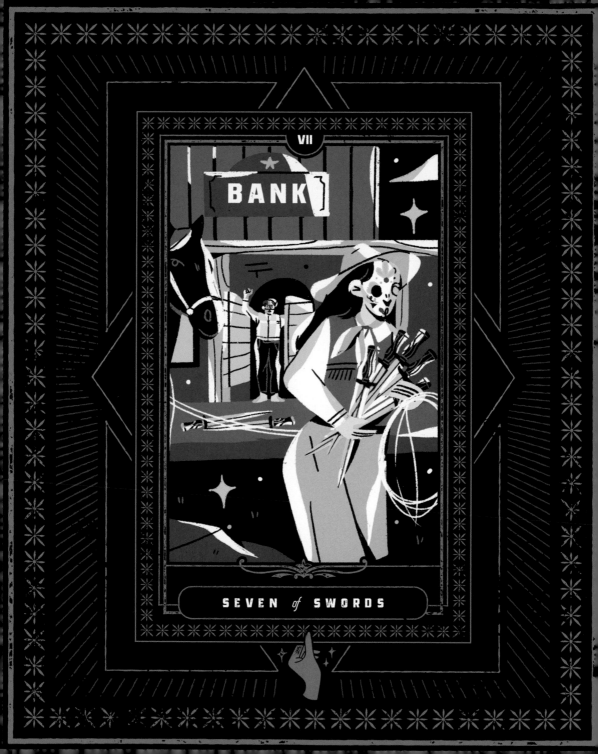

# *The* SEVEN *of* SWORDS

✳✳✳✳✳✳✳✳✳✳✳✳✳✳✳✳✳✳✳✳✳✳✳✳✳✳✳✳✳✳✳✳✳✳

## BASIC DEFINITION

The Seven of Swords usually refers to a theft of some kind. Is someone being deceptive with you? Regardless of what it is, this card most often has someone getting away with something. You have to be strategic and stealthy with your interactions, because if you are not, they may be taken the wrong way. There is an aspect of partial success/partial loss when talking about this card because the person stealing something may *want* to be found out. You can only keep secrets for so long until the weight becomes crushing.

## TEQUILA DEFINITION

You know that friend of yours who gets away without having to pay for a single drink the entire night? How do they do it? It's almost strategic. You sit back and watch your friend stroll up to the bar, recover two drinks, and then come walking back with a mischievous smile on their face. You ask them how much you owe for the drinks and they say, "Don't worry about it, I didn't pay for them." You can't imagine your friend being deceptive, but then again, you could be wrong.

## *Reversed* BASIC DEFINITION

The Seven of Swords Reversed still speaks to deceit, but usually the theft refers to you lying to yourself. This card can also mean that you are done being sneaky and looking to find the truth in all you seek to clear your conscience. Maybe you have come clean about something that you have stolen, or someone admitted a theft to you. Justice will find a way of making itself known with the Seven of Swords Reversed.

## *Reversed* TEQUILA DEFINITION

Sometimes you become a beacon of truth when you've had one too many. That last drink is like a truth serum. Clearing your conscience makes you feel better and so does unburdening your secrets onto those we love. There is always the risk they won't take it well; however, at least you took the high road. If you feel you have to lie to someone in order to get closer to them, guess what? It wasn't meant to be.

*Something's missing in your relationship. You can feel it. Is it the way they're acting toward you? Did you find a sign of infidelity? Was something stolen from you?*

*Your mind is rushing to find a semblance of tranquility in the midst of this mental chaos. You grab your partner and head into the kitchen. The teapot is screaming for answers, and so are you. You pour this blue-colored drink into two glasses and stare into your partner's eyes. Blue is a color of trust and wisdom. Blue is the color of a beautiful sky. Let this cocktail be your truth serum. Hopefully, your partner won't notice you're both sitting among blue and white candles; we wouldn't want to give the whole "ritual" away.*

*Loose lips can sink ships, but they can also reveal truths. As you're both locking eyes, ask your questions and let your intuition decide if the other is lying or not. If you're not sure after the first drink, pour another. You're bound to get an answer after a couple of cocktails.*

*Serve in* ╱ *a collins glass*

# The
# SEVEN OF SWORDS COCKTAIL

### 1 1/2 OUNCES SILVER TEQUILA

### 1/2 OUNCE COINTREAU

### 1 OUNCE FRESH LEMON JUICE

### 1/2 OUNCE HONEY SIMPLE SYRUP [SEE PAGE 43]

### 2 OUNCES BUTTERFLY PEA FLOWER TEA [RECIPE FOLLOWS]

### ZEST OF 1 LEMON, FOR GARNISH

✦

*Add all the ingredients, except the tea, to a shaker filled with ice. Shake thoroughly, then pour the cocktail into a collins glass. Slowly add the tea to the top of the cocktail, giving a colorful layered effect. Garnish with the lemon zest.*

#### BUTTERFLY PEA FLOWER TEA

*Steep 2 bags of butterfly pea flower tea using a tea strainer basket or simply wrapping the tea in a cheesecloth. Chill overnight and keep in the refrigerator for up to two weeks.*

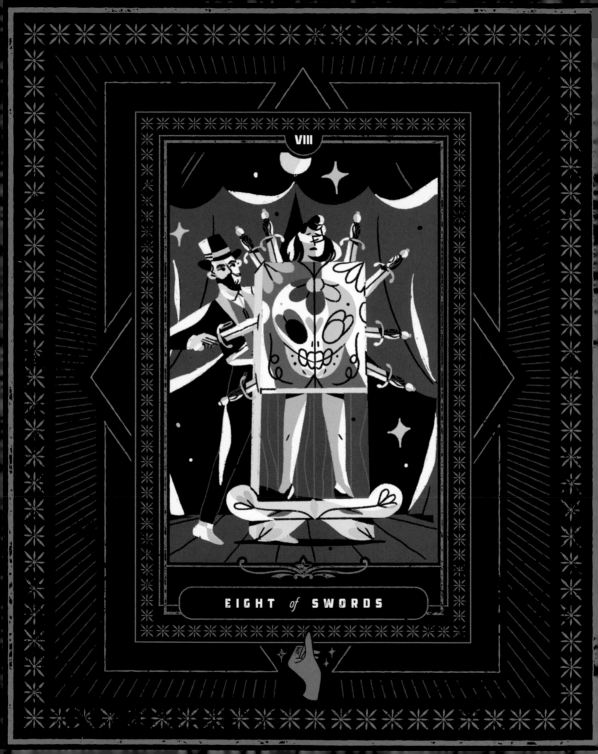

# The EIGHT of SWORDS

✳︎✳︎✳︎✳︎✳︎✳︎✳︎✳︎✳︎✳︎✳︎✳︎✳︎✳︎✳︎✳︎✳︎✳︎✳︎✳︎✳︎✳︎✳︎✳︎✳︎✳︎✳︎✳︎✳︎

## BASIC DEFINITION

The Eight of Swords looks worse than it is. The primary message of this card is that you're feeling trapped by self-doubt and fear. You're feeling mentally bound. The secret to overcoming this card is realizing that no one is restraining you but yourself. The minute you see this, you've taken the first step toward your own freedom. The Eight of Swords also reminds you of the many options you have when faced with a seemingly hopeless situation. Especially when you feel like you have none. When you're paralyzed by confusion, use the time to reflect and open your eyes to see things for how they really are, not how you perceive them.

## *Reversed* BASIC DEFINITION

The Eight of Swords Reversed refers to the liberation and awakening that happens once you figure out that you have the courage to trust yourself and see beyond the fear that has been affecting you. Another interpretation of the Eight of Swords Reversed is that you see yourself as a victim and feel helpless. This is a good time to mention that any card can mean different things based on the question being asked during a reading, as well as what the other cards that are surrounding it in the spread are indicating. See this card as an awakening; however, if the other cards are negative, the victim mentality might well be what we talk about.

## TEQUILA DEFINITION

Can you break free from the mental ties that bind you? Stressing about your forward mobility can make anyone feel like they are going nowhere. We place these limitations on ourselves and remain trapped in our own confusion until we can see the truth for what it really is. And the truth is that we are free to live our best lives at any moment we choose! We just need to lift our heads off the bar and open our eyes to what's really happening around us.

## *Reversed* TEQUILA DEFINITION

Not every relationship will be like your last one. Sure, it ended quite badly, but you need to release yourself from the past and trust in yourself again. You have to look beyond the painful breakup and give in to the feeling of a new potential love. You are not a victim! Your ex was a total drag when it came to power and manipulation, but that is all in the past now. You woke up one day to see them for who they really were and that got you packing. No more mental shackles—you are free!

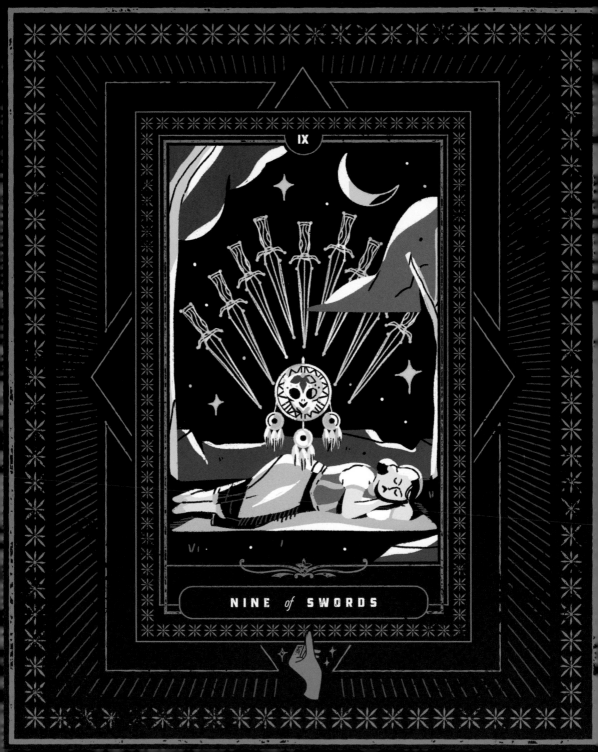

# The NINE of SWORDS

✳✳✳✳✳✳✳✳✳✳✳✳✳✳✳✳✳✳✳✳✳✳✳✳✳✳✳✳✳✳✳✳

## BASIC DEFINITION

This anxiety-filled card reminds us to only worry about what we can actively control. The main definition speaks to imagined concerns, feeling overwhelmed, and distress. This card also represents the inability to get a good night's sleep and/or having nightmares. Life is hard enough as it is without adding annoying, irrational thoughts on top of it. It's not worth worrying about things that we do not have any control over or that aren't real.

## Reversed BASIC DEFINITION

The Nine of Swords Reversed teaches us that through mindfulness and conscious decisions we can overcome the worries and difficulties that have been making us anxious. You are able to recognize where your anxiety and stress have been coming from and have started on the road to recovery. You see the confusion lifting and the nights are becoming a little easier to deal with. If this card is surrounded by more negative cards, there is a chance we could be talking about unrealized fears and the inability to come to terms with your obsessive worrying. But for the most part, this card shows that you can change your thought patterns if you try.

## TEQUILA DEFINITION

Some people drink to feel happy, while others drink to help them go to sleep or to dull the worries that have been plaguing them. It's a crippling cycle. Tequila won't make you sleep better, and it won't make the pain go away. We have to become accountable for our own problems, and if they are becoming too much for us then we need to seek counseling to help us through. Don't look to the bottle as an opportunity to find courage, you already have it.

## Reversed TEQUILA DEFINITION

When the haze of a hangover washes away and you pour that first coffee of the morning, you start to see a way out of the cloudiness. You start thinking logically, and the self-doubt you've been carrying inside you is evaporating. There is a feeling of paranoia that you did something stupid the night before, so you call a friend in hopes of quieting the inner turmoil making you pace. Luckily, you are relieved to find out that it was all in your mind and you behaved yourself. Once again, you overthought everything but, because you were thinking clearly, you found a way out by actively communicating your concerns.

# *The* TEN *of* SWORDS

✴✴✴✴✴✴✴✴✴✴✴✴✴✴✴✴✴✴✴✴✴✴✴✴✴✴✴✴✴✴✴✴✴✴✴

## BASIC DEFINITION

When the Ten of Swords shows up in a reading, it is very safe to say something has come to an end. Most often the ending is painful, like someone stabbed you in the back or you were betrayed by a good friend. The Ten of Swords talks of times when you are in a crisis. However, whenever you are dealing with a crisis, there is always a chance to find healing, resilience, and a new opportunity. The hard lesson of the Ten of Swords is that in order to progress through the pain you need to forgive and surrender. That is the only way you can truly break clean from the misfortune you've been carrying.

## *Reversed* BASIC DEFINITION

Look closely at the visual representation on the Ten of Swords. Do you see the dawn breaking far off in the background? That's because a main definition of this card is that whatever has ended is over, and now we can focus on the start of a new day. The Ten of Swords Reversed can also mean avoiding a crisis or being restored and/or transformed after battling through the painful ending you just experienced. Depending on whether there are more problematic cards around it, the Ten of Swords Reversed can mean hitting rock bottom and being faced with a devastating loss. If the cards surrounding it are more positive, then it can mean recovery.

## TEQUILA DEFINITION

It's a sad day. Your favorite watering hole has burned to the ground, and they say there may be foul play attached to it. This was one of those town bars that you could walk to. There were no bad vibes at all. You walked in and people greeted you like you were family. There's no coming back from this. Even if the owner put up a new establishment in its place, it wouldn't be the same . . . but maybe it could be better?

## *Reversed* TEQUILA DEFINITION

Your friend finally showed their true colors and, instead of lashing out, you resisted and decided to chalk it up to a lesson learned. Sure, it'll be hard to trust that person again, and you may not want to for a while, which is fine. Eventually the sun will rise and all of the past problems you have had to deal with will be over. Even bad things have to come to an end, right? Consider yourself lucky! You avoided any further problems with this person by ending the relationship immediately and not holding on to the feelings of a victim.

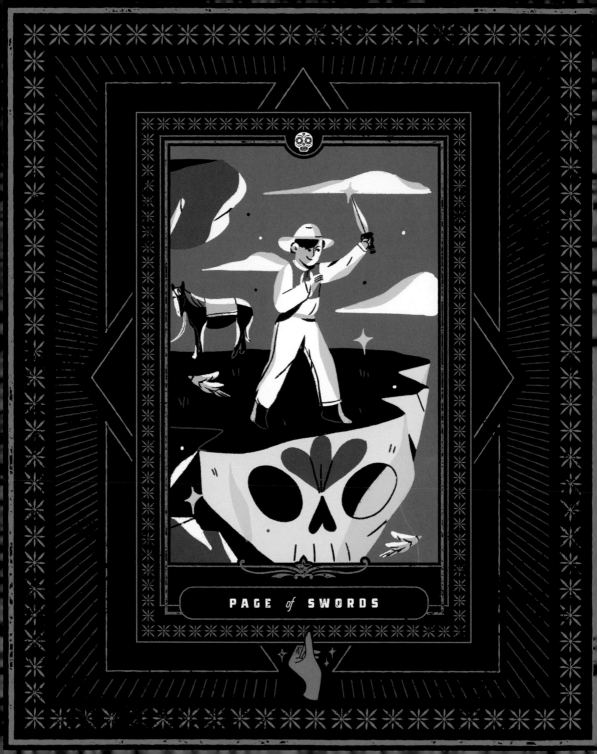

PAGE *of* SWORDS

# The PAGE of SWORDS

✳✳✳✳✳✳✳✳✳✳✳✳✳✳✳✳✳✳✳✳✳✳✳✳✳✳✳✳✳✳✳✳

## BASIC DEFINITION

The Page of Swords, if talking about a person, describes someone having a lot of restless energy and ideas. They have a thirst to learn new things and a curiosity that can sometimes get them into trouble. If not talking about a person, this card can be speaking about an intellectual pursuit. It's possible you just got notified about a college acceptance. The message can be referring to any important or unexpected news.

## *Reversed* BASIC DEFINITION

When that eager student becomes too annoying to put up with or when gossip has gotten a bit out of control, the energy of the Page of Swords Reversed is whirling past you. People just aren't good at communicating. Some folks are all talk and no action, while others hurt you with childlike cruelty. They laugh when you fall on your face or fail at something you love. The Page of Swords Reversed wants you to believe the lies and the bullshit.

## TEQUILA DEFINITION

After years of not being satisfied with your current place in the world, you've decided to go back to school and further your education. You've always felt stifled, like you couldn't speak your mind, and that has frustrated you. Maybe communications or marketing would allow your true nature to shine. Maybe you can create an ad campaign for that popular tequila you love so much?

## *Reversed* TEQUILA DEFINITION

You were never more embarrassed in all of your life. Your friend insisted on being your wingman because he so desperately wanted you to find someone special. He said he'd put himself last and just be there for you. You didn't believe it when he said it, but after the fiasco that just went down you learned a valuable lesson in trust. He spent the whole evening making up stories to the women you were talking to because he wanted them to be impressed with you. Was it the tequila talking, or was it just him being a little too over the top? The lies spewing from his mouth make him look like a complete fraud. Even if you had found someone you liked, he ruined your chance.

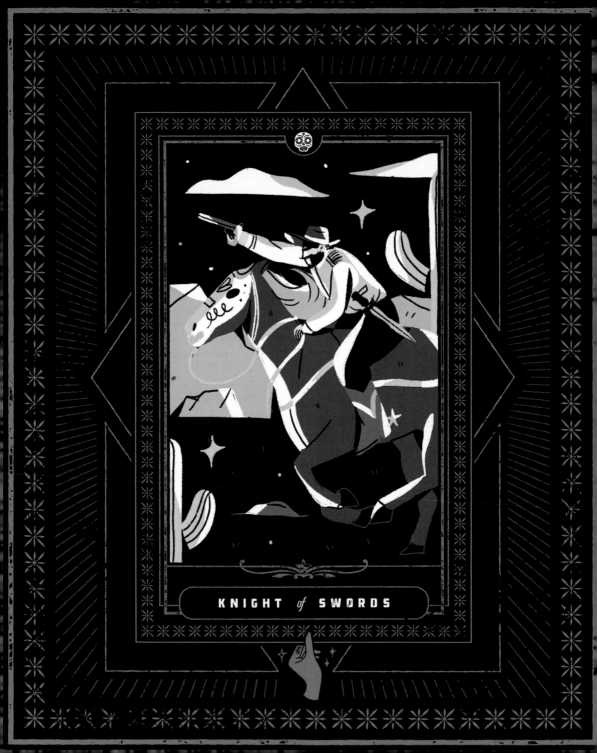

KNIGHT *of* SWORDS

# The KNIGHT of SWORDS

✳✳✳✳✳✳✳✳✳✳✳✳✳✳✳✳✳✳✳✳✳✳✳✳✳✳✳✳✳✳

## BASIC DEFINITION

When the Knight of Swords enters the picture, you can expect rapid change. Life sometimes calls for bold solutions and determination in order to the save the day. And this Knight, in particular, excels at that. He may be a bit intense and hyper-focused. And sure, he's a bit reactive in his pursuit for excellence, which can come off as a bit obsessive, but all he really wants to do is fix the problem and move on to the next one. Line them up and knock them down!

## *Reversed* BASIC DEFINITION

The Knight of Swords Reversed is often impatient and reckless. They may get caught up in a whirlwind of thought and chaotic energy, so much so that they will start to behave in a very unpredictable manner to get something resolved. A lot of times, when the reversed Knight appears in a reading, there may be more damage added to the cards that have already been spread out.

## TEQUILA DEFINITION

Your friend hates the phrase "all talk and no action" because he firmly believes he does both. Direct with his communication and following up on all promises made, his ambitious and assertive nature always has the best of intentions. He didn't mean to start that fight at the concert the other night, but he felt that those guys with the vulgar mouths were being a bit too rude to his girlfriend. And that did not sit well with him at all.

## *Reversed* TEQUILA DEFINITION

Have you ever been swept away in a very angry crowd while attending a heavy metal concert? The force and chaos around you can lift you up and can knock you down. It can knock you into another person and cause serious damage to you and others. It's a force of unstable energy that is also unreliable and scattered, leading to a lot of thoughtless and impulsive actions. I picture a thousand excitable reversed Knights flying around a mosh pit without a care in the world about who they crash into.

QUEEN *of* SWORDS

# The QUEEN of SWORDS

✳✳✳✳✳✳✳✳✳✳✳✳✳✳✳✳✳✳✳✳✳✳✳✳✳✳✳✳✳✳✳✳✳✳✳

## BASIC DEFINITION

The Queen of Swords, at her best, is highly intelligent. She's powerful, clever, and quick-witted. This man or woman can be of wise and logical counsel and can offer you great wisdom if you take her advice. The Queen of Swords is a seeker and giver of truth. You will have no problem understanding her ability to communicate her needs and wants. She would make a great lawyer and educator. If we are not talking about a particular person, the Queen of Swords can mean that you need to draw upon her attributes to help you navigate a situation.

## *Reversed* BASIC DEFINITION

The Queen of Swords Reversed often describes a cold communicator. This person can be so emotionally detached that they come across like an ice queen. They can be argumentative to the point of being cruel. They can be aloof and seemingly apathetic. If not referring to a person, the Queen of Swords Reversed can point out that maybe you are being a little harsh or judgmental with someone and you should look inside yourself to see if you are being misinterpreted. It's true: Sometimes we need to be forceful in order to get our point across. But at what expense and cost to others?

## TEQUILA DEFINITION

When the bartender asks you what type of tequila you want in your margarita, tell them! Don't just say, "Whatever tequila you have." Put a name to that margarita. Don't be afraid to be as direct as you need to be. The bartender wants you to be happy. It's okay to speak your truth if it helps you attain your desires.

## *Reversed* TEQUILA DEFINITION

The bar is packed and patrons are being downright rude to one another. The bartenders are ignoring you to the point where you start pushing your way to the front to be noticed. Still not getting shown the attention you feel that you deserve, you lash out with some bitter words in order to be heard. However, the minute you yelled at the bartenders you realize how you probably came across. No one likes to be barked at. Unfortunately, the mean-spirited Queen of Swords Reversed will continue her ways until someone strong enough calls her out on her behavior.

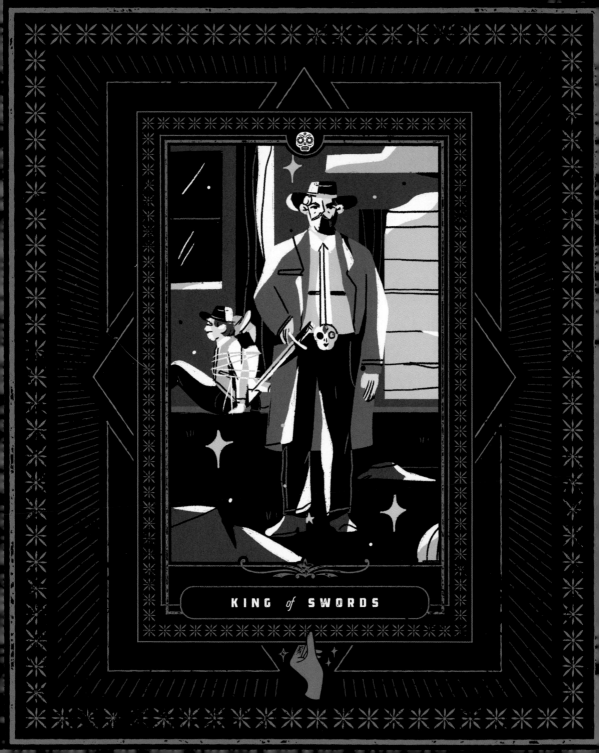

KING *of* SWORDS

# The KING of SWORDS

## BASIC DEFINITION

A strong leader, the King of Swords is someone who's in a position of authority. This person uses logic to find the truth. They may be a fair decision maker and one who delivers harsh but sound advice. If this does not represent someone you know, then it can represent an aspect of your personality. The King of Swords is a thinker; they may not be the most emotional person you'll meet, but that doesn't mean they don't feel.

## Reversed BASIC DEFINITION

When power and authority become manipulative and abusive, you may be experiencing some King of Swords Reversed energy. Some people have a tendency to micromanage a situation whether it's because they are power hungry or they have their own personal agendas. What can you do when you face a person like this? They are so stubborn and rigid in their opinions that they will probably never come around to your way of thinking. This person may even be a threat to your happiness or livelihood. The only way for this person to like or trust you is if you are a messenger of truth—to the point where there will be no misunderstandings from your intentions.

## TEQUILA DEFINITION

When the night gets a bit out of hand and the manager of the establishment asks you to leave, he's not making it personal. Within this place of business, he is the authority figure and what he/she says goes. At this point, there's no chance talking him out of his decision. The damage was done and he has his mind set on following through. Even though you feel you were treated unfairly, you know that, unfortunately, the night has come to an end. And, chances are, tomorrow, you'll be regretting your actions.

## Reversed TEQUILA DEFINITION

The micromanaging restaurant owner is a great representation of the King of Swords Reversed. This person will drive you crazy with his or her inability to trust you to do your job correctly. If you show any resistance to their authority, they will probably make up a reason to let you go. Other negative attributes can be showing off, selfishness, and unreasonableness. Maybe this wasn't the perfect job for you after all.

# The
# MYSTICAL PAIRING

What can you say about the simple peanut? Did you know it represents longevity, growth, and good fortune? The peanut is just one component of this cocktail aimed at improving your overall confidence, maturity, and feelings of security.

On a night before a job interview, a court case, or anything regarding issues of authority and/or security, this will be your go-to drink. Embodying the strength of the King of Swords helps us to gain much needed clarity and intellect. When you need to make a well-thought-out decision without our pesky hearts getting in the way, select a quiet place in your house to meditate. Light a white candle to clear the negativity and light some cinnamon incense to comfort you. Make sure your quartz crystals are charged (see page xiv) and start sipping your cocktail. As the ritual starts to take hold, add some positive affirmations. Let the universe know what you need and don't be afraid to ask for help.

*Serve in* a rocks glass

# The
# KING OF SWORDS COCKTAIL

---

3 OUNCES PEANUT-INFUSED BULLEIT BOURBON [RECIPE FOLLOWS]

1 OUNCE WHITE CRÈME DE COCOA

1/2 OUNCE SKREWBALL WHISKEY

4 DASHES AZTEC CHOCOLATE BITTERS

ORANGE PEEL, FOR GARNISH [FLAME OPTIONAL; SEE PAGE 9]

BRANDIED CHERRY, FOR GARNISH

✦

*Add all of the contents into a mixing glass filled with ice. Stir 12 times each way until a noticeable condensation occurs outside the glass. Strain over a rocks glass with a large ice block. Garnish with a large zest of orange and a brandied cherry.*

### PEANUT-INFUSED BULLEIT BOURBON

*Add Bulleit Bourbon to a jar, leaving about three ounces on top. Add peanut oil to fill. Cap the jar and store in the fridge for 5 days, giving the jar a shake every other day. Place the jar in the freezer for a day (this separates the fat from the bourbon). Finally, strain the remaining bourbon into a second jar.*

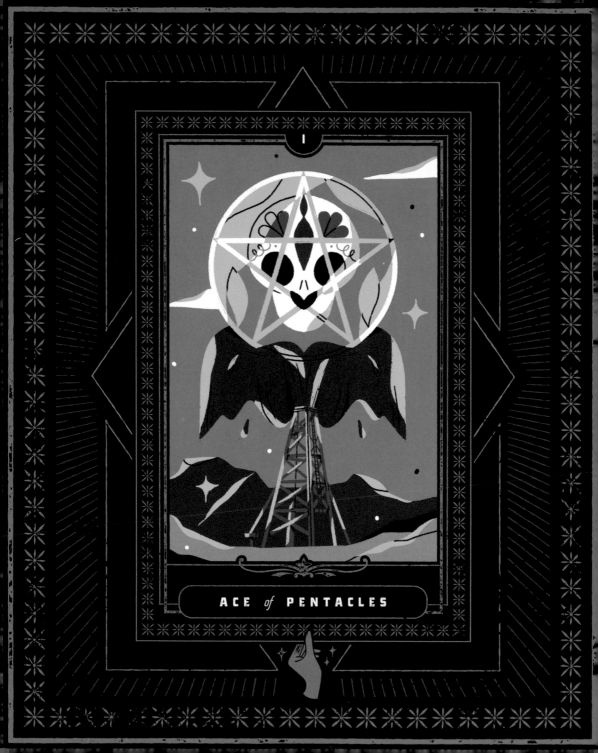

ACE *of* PENTACLES

# The ACE of PENTACLES

✳✳✳✳✳✳✳✳✳✳✳✳✳✳✳✳✳✳✳✳✳✳✳✳✳✳✳✳✳✳✳✳✳✳✳

## BASIC DEFINITION

The Ace of Pentacles shows the start of something new. All of the aces represent beginnings; however, this particular ace speaks of material gain and abundance. It could be a new job offer will be coming your way or, perhaps, you will get an opportunity in your current position for a great financial success, or you'll reach a new financial goal. The Ace of Pentacles can indicate that you will be receiving a windfall of money from somewhere unexpected, or it could also mean that you are planning to move your residence or make an investment into your current home's improvement or additions.

## *Reversed* BASIC DEFINITION

The Ace of Pentacles Reversed can warn of financial hardships or poor budgeting. You can look at this card as still being positive, just that the positives will be delayed. This card can also mean that you are focusing too much on the material side of life and may need to reprioritize your true goals. The Ace of Pentacles Reversed shows a need to be grounded; you may have a tendency to become overanxious if your finances are not in order. Remember, wealth does not always lead to happiness.

## TEQUILA DEFINITION

You just received some money that was owed to you and it was really needed. Your life has been on hold for a while, but you've had a plan brewing for years. The long-term goal? Own a restaurant. The short-term goal? Maybe a food truck to help get your name and brand out there. This newfound money will be used for planting the seeds of your future. It will lead to growth and an opportunity to build and create something new for you and your family for years to come.

## *Reversed* TEQUILA DEFINITION

You have a need for all things luxurious. The renovation of your home wasn't the smartest decision, you'll admit, but you thought creating a bar in your man cave would impress your friends and everyone would want to spend more time with you there. You spent a lot of additional money on the high-end tequilas and other spirits to showcase in your bar. This was always a dream of yours; however, it wasn't very practical. You overextended your spending on this project and it's not even finished yet.

# *The* MYSTICAL PAIRING

*Lying in the grass, shaded underneath a tall billowy birch tree, you are reminded that we are all connected to nature and should strive to be at one with it. Mist floats around you, as if you are wrapped in a cloud. The Ace of Pentacles brings the hope of earthly success. It says, putting in the GROUNDwork and the planning will soon manifest into what you aspire to achieve.*

*Combine the earthly powers of birch, rye, bitters, absinthe, and star anise to ritualize this new start with a beverage. After the ingredients are in your glass, stir twelve times in each direction. The creativity of the number twelve also has the power to bring forth the physical to the spiritual and vice versa. Spraying the absinthe into the glass further awakens your senses and grounds you so you can raise this cocktail to your lips and fulfill your earthly desires. Call upon your friends and drink together, making the ritual stronger!*

*Serve in* ⟍ ⟋ *a rocks glass*

# *The*
# ACE OF PENTACLES COCKTAIL

2 OUNCES STRAIGHT RYE

1/2 OUNCE BIRCH SIMPLE SYRUP [RECIPE FOLLOWS]

5 DASHES PEYCHAUD BITTERS

2 DASHES ANGOSTURA BITTERS

1/4 OUNCE ST. GEORGE ABSINTHE, IN A SPRAY BOTTLE

1 STAR ANISE, FOR GARNISH

✦

*Add the rye, birch simple syrup, and bitters to a mixing glass with ice and stir 12 times in each direction. Spray the rocks glass with the absinthe mist. Serve the cocktail up (no ice) and garnish with a star anise.*

### BIRCH SIMPLE SYRUP

*Place 1 cup birch bark, 1 cup sugar, and 1 cup water in a saucepan and bring to a rolling boil. Once the sugar has dissolved, strain out the birch bark by pouring your syrup through a fine strainer. Add optional wintergreen leaves, anise, and juniper berries to enhance the flavor.*

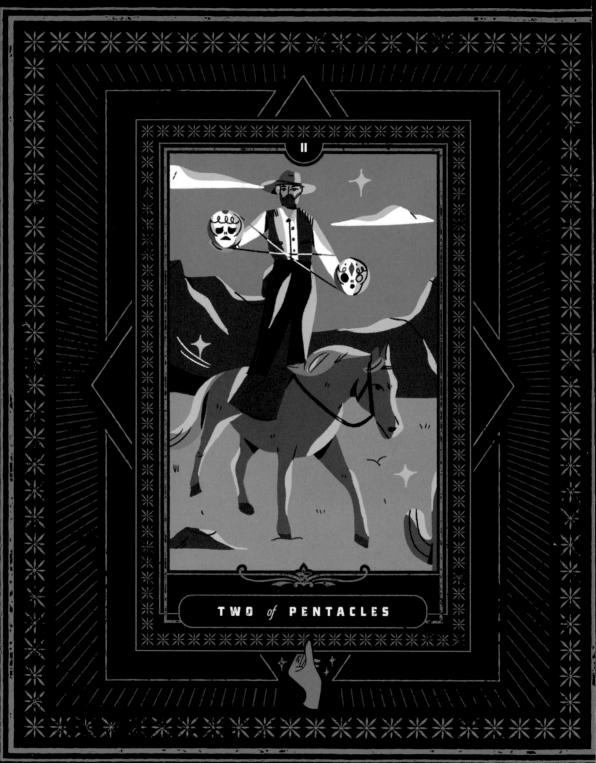

TWO *of* PENTACLES

# The TWO of PENTACLES

## BASIC DEFINITION

The Two of Pentacles explains the desperate need for balance that we all struggle with on a daily basis. It reminds us that we need to be flexible in our daily affairs and that, instead of juggling our responsibilities, we actually take them on one by one and get them done. The Two of Pentacles also means that you need to make a choice but can't think clearly for some reason and are struggling to find clarity. You may feel like you're walking on a tightrope, and balance is not your friend. But don't be so hard on yourself. You're actually keeping your head above water and taking care of your responsibilities.

## *Reversed* BASIC DEFINITION

There is a feeling of instability with the Two of Pentacles Reversed. The card asks you to look within yourself and find out what led to this feeling so you can now attempt to fix it. Was it too many choices that left you inactive? Were you committing to too many things? Maybe you've just become reckless and you now need to slow down. When this card shows up in a reading, find the harmony and balance you've misplaced and use it to restore your equilibrium.

## TEQUILA DEFINITION

Every day of your life, you are called to wear many different hats. You are the parent that has the full-time job. You are the primary caregiver for your children. You still like to go out and let loose from time to time, even though it's getting increasingly hard to do so. Managing your income, adhering to your budget, and paying bills has your head spinning. Your friends are impressed that you can manage by yourself; however, you feel like the balancing act you've been walking can't last forever. Maybe you're being too hard on yourself? Whatever you do, don't add tequila to the equation.

## *Reversed* TEQUILA DEFINITION

You can't live your life the way you want to when you are running around like a chicken with its head cut off. You know you're out of balance. You have put so much of your time into your job that your home life is being neglected. Your spouse and kids say you're never around. And yes, you do feel guilty. But what can you do? You have become inundated with work and your once balanced scales have become completely weighed down on one side. You know you need to slow down, but your business will fall apart without you being there. At least that's what you *think* will happen. Pouring yourself an añejo neat might just be what you need to calm those nerves.

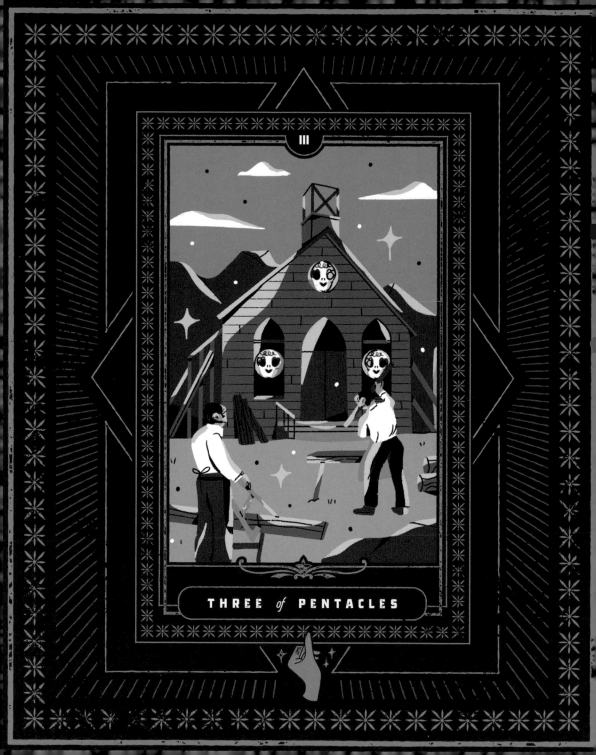

# The **THREE** of **PENTACLES**

## BASIC DEFINITION

The Three of Pentacles is the card of teamwork and collaboration. If you are planning on starting a project with your friends, family, or business associates, then it will be a great success. It's truly a blessing when multiple people can come together and have that magical synergy. Everyone is respectful of each other's opinions, and everyone brings their own skills and resources to the table to make it completely cooperative.

## *Reversed* BASIC DEFINITION

The opposite of the Three of Pentacles is true here. Instead of being a part of a perfect, mutually respectful team, you are stuck in a group of people who are at each other's throats. Whether it's because of competition, selfishness, or ego, the Three of Pentacles Reversed says you would rather go it alone right now. This particular reversed three also speaks to craftsmanship that is not done up to snuff. Are you rushing a project to completion without the proper training or resources? Are you merely concerned about getting the job done so you'll get paid, while everything else suffers for it?

## TEQUILA DEFINITION

It's not easy being in a three-person band. There's no place to hide. There is no second guitar or keyboard to fill up the sound. It's just you and your two friends trying to be as unique and creative as can be with what you have. You're lucky to be teamed with like-minded individuals who work well together and get along. The sky's the limit on what you all can manifest and create—a true group effort to be excited about!

## *Reversed* TEQUILA DEFINITION

It just so happens that there are three local bars in your town and they all seem to be competing with each other instead of listening to the needs of the community and working together. There are more than enough people to frequent all these establishments, and there are more than enough bands to play there, too. When each separate location seems to be pushing its own agenda, the power struggle between owners is easily seen by the employees, and even the patrons. Maybe instead of going it alone, you can pull together and do some great things for the community. Just because you have similar businesses doesn't mean you have to be threatened by one another.

# The
# MYSTICAL PAIRING

*Whether you're in a band creating music or you have a group presentation due in college, the Three of Pentacles is the card you want to see when you're hoping for a positive outcome. It's the card of teamwork and good craftsmanship.*

*When you are looking for that extra edge to make sure your team project or that carpenter you just hired does a great job, hammer out this recipe (not literally). The night before the work commences or the night before you present a finished project follow this simple ritual.*

*Prepare your cocktail and set it on a workbench or some table you've created or cared for. Place the potion between two lit green candles. Encircle the glass with crystals of jade and moonstones and place three silver dollars in front of you. Meditate on the project coming out perfectly and, once you can visualize the successful outcome, blow out the candles. If you are part of a team, invite your partners over for some extra empowerment; just make sure you have enough bourbon.*

*Serve in*     *a double rocks glass*

# *The*
# THREE OF PENTACLES COCKTAIL

**3 1/2 OUNCES FIG-INFUSED FOUR ROSES BOURBON** [RECIPE FOLLOWS]

**4 DASHES ANGOSTURA BITTERS**

**1/2 OUNCE HONEY SIMPLE SYRUP** [SEE PAGE 43]

**ORANGE PEEL, FOR GARNISH** [FLAME OPTIONAL; SEE PAGE 9]

**1 DRIED FIG, FOR GARNISH**

✦

*Add the bourbon, bitters, and honey syrup to a mixing glass and stir 12 times in each direction until condensation occurs on the outside of the glass. Strain over a big ice cube in a double rocks glass and garnish with a large zest of orange and dried fig.*

### FIG-INFUSED FOUR ROSES BOURBON

*Please 6 dried figs in a jar and fill with Four Roses bourbon. Set aside on a shelf at room temperature for a week. The infusion will deepen in flavor with time.*

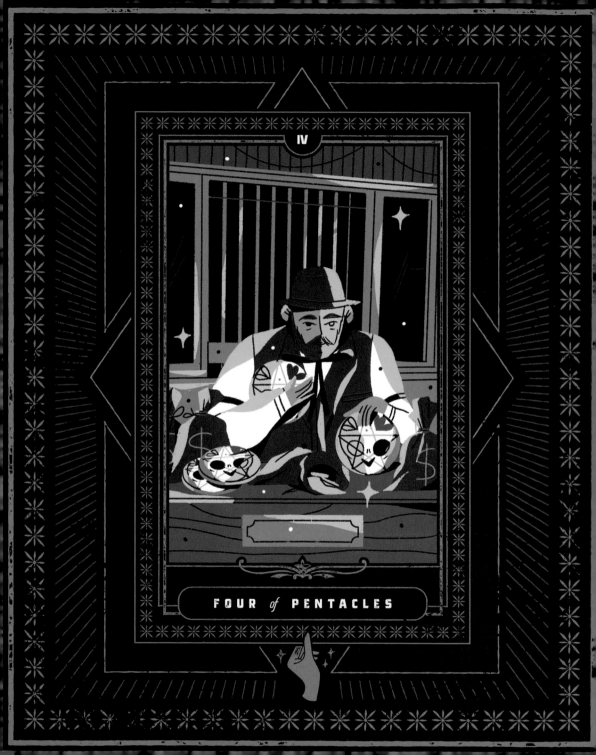

FOUR *of* PENTACLES

# The **FOUR** of **PENTACLES**

## BASIC DEFINITION

The Four of Pentacles says you have reached a point in your life when you have accumulated significant savings and stability. You are in a position to help people in need and be a little generous. Don't let your fear of having the right amount get in the way of your spending some of that money on things that will make you happy. There is a possessiveness about this card that may make you want to stay indoors and hide—maybe you are too controlling of your finances or too conservative with you're spending to ever fully allow yourself to go out and have a good time.

## *Reversed* BASIC DEFINITION

The Four of Pentacles Reversed asks you to look at your relationship with your money and see if you are putting too much value on it. Are you hoarding your wealth for a rainy day? Have you become too miserly and frugal with your spending? Maybe it's time to be more charitable now that you can afford it. Maybe leaving your comfort zone and giving a little more of yourself, both financially and lovingly, will bring clarity to what you value most.

## TEQUILA DEFINITION

You just spent a few hundred dollars on this premium, rare, hard-to-find tequila. You have coveted this purchase for so long, so you only bring it out on such rare occasions like a lunar eclipse. Your friends joke with you about your special purchase. They ask if they can try a sip, knowing that you will never part with even a little. You would prefer going out to a bar and buying your friends a round of shots just to get their prying eyes away from your precious tequila. Maybe you do put a little too much value in materialistic things.

## *Reversed* TEQUILA DEFINITION

We all have that one friend who needs a little extra attention from us. They always put up a struggle about leaving their house to go anywhere. It's not like they can't afford it; they are actually pretty well off. They genuinely choose to be unattached and alone with the things that make them most happy: their possessions. Maybe they are selfish and too materialistic, but you have also known them to be generous at times. You keep telling them that they are missing out on the exciting things in life by never leaving the comfort of their four walls. Never feeling connected to others because they've made a conscious choice to place more power on those things they can purchase and thus control.

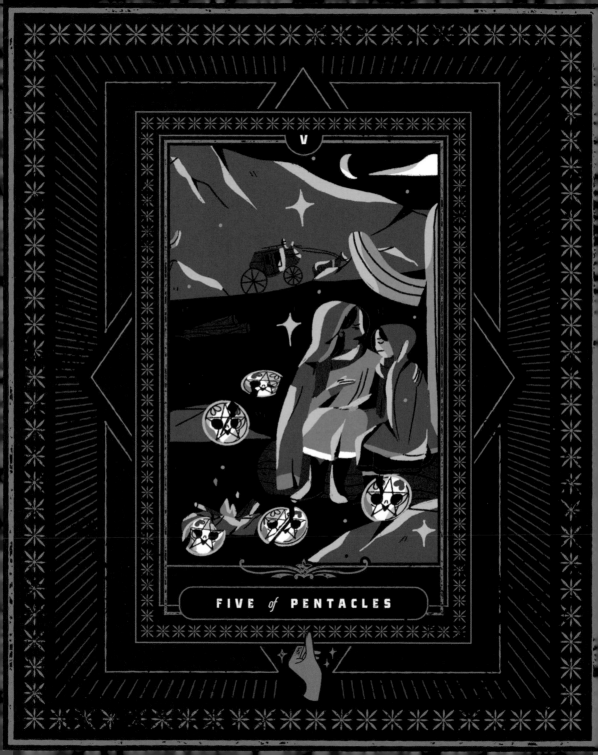

# The FIVE of PENTACLES

✳✳✳✳✳✳✳✳✳✳✳✳✳✳✳✳✳✳✳✳✳✳✳✳✳✳✳✳✳✳✳✳✳✳✳✳✳

## BASIC DEFINITION

When the Five of Pentacles shows up in a reading, be prepared to go through a difficult time. Usually this card refers to the misfortune of finances, but it can also speak to relationships and health issues. The Five of Pentacles brings with it a sense of abandonment and feeling like you've been excommunicated from your church. Once you can recover from the feelings of self-pity, you can take this as a lesson for spiritual strength and growth.

## *Reversed* BASIC DEFINITION

The Five of Pentacles Reversed is actually better in this position than its right-side-up counterpart. Reversed, it talks about financial recovery and rebuilding the wealth that you may have lost. Either way, this card says you've been through the worst of times and thankfully the future looks brighter. It's important to stop feeling destitute and worthless because that time is over. You can now focus on moving forward with positivity.

## TEQUILA DEFINITION

You've clearly fallen on hard times. It was one obstacle after another that led you to drinking away all your problems only to find that by doing so you've created a bunch of new ones. You have two options: You can start working the program and accept the help that has always been right in front of you, or you can continue feeling isolated and like a social outcast. You have more of a choice than you know.

## *Reversed* TEQUILA DEFINITION

Recovery comes in many forms. You can choose the path of spiritual enlightenment or you can choose to follow a more traditional religious route. After drinking yourself to a rock-bottom low, you finally see the light at the end of the tunnel. You can proceed with a life of clean living and follow the golden rule. This renewed courage and strength has entered your life with a new sense of self-worth. You will not allow yourself to continue blocking your forward momentum. You now have the peace of mind you have been looking for, and there is no way you are going to throw it away.

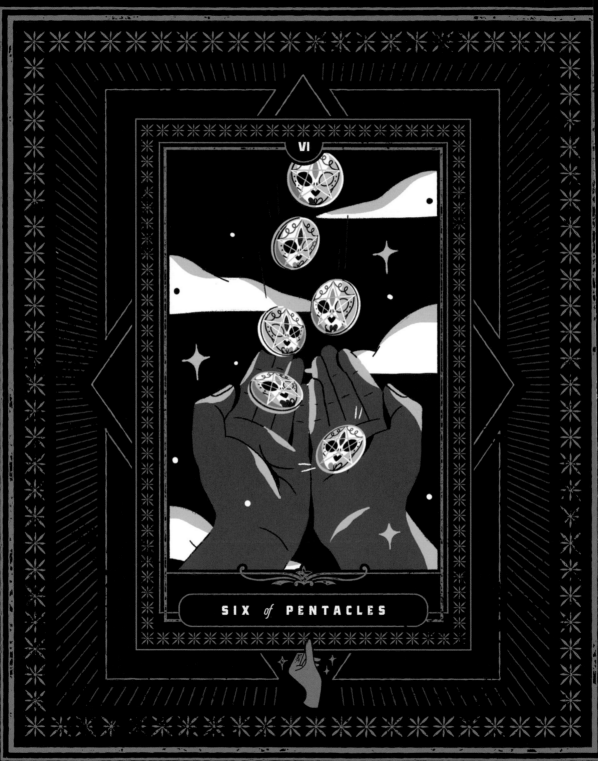

VI

SIX *of* PENTACLES

# *The* SIX *of* PENTACLES

✳︎✳︎✳︎✳︎✳︎✳︎✳︎✳︎✳︎✳︎✳︎✳︎✳︎✳︎✳︎✳︎✳︎✳︎✳︎✳︎✳︎✳︎✳︎✳︎✳︎✳︎✳︎✳︎

## BASIC DEFINITION

The Six of Pentacles is a card of charity and helping others when they need it. Any great relationship has two people who both give and receive freely, without any ulterior motives. When this card shows up in a reading it might be telling you to be charitable and generous with what you have. Just as you would appreciate help from someone else, you too can return a favor. The Six of Pentacles can identify with any type of relationship, whether it be love, work, or family.

## TEQUILA DEFINITION

There are many small local companies that can use your support. If you believe in them, let them know! You don't have to be wealthy to be charitable; you can help out in your own way. I'm sure there are tequila start-ups right now looking for investors. Go make someone feel good and support a local project.

## *Reversed* BASIC DEFINITION

The Six of Pentacles Reversed defines the typical selfish relationship where one person is giving and the other is taking. This card also refers to being uncharitable and not choosing to help others in need. Perhaps you aren't able or wanting to receive help either. The act of charity should not come with conditions, nor should any healthy relationship. The Six of Pentacles Reversed asks us to examine the relationships we are in. Are they equal, or do you find yourself the victim of an unbalanced union?

## *Reversed* TEQUILA DEFINITION

You can learn a lot about your friends when you're out drinking together. Think about who you can rely on to be the designated driver. Who is the person who you can never rely on to pick up a round of tequila shots, or who will always offer to pick up the tab? Wouldn't it be wonderful if everyone kept it all balanced? If you find yourself having to pay for more than your fair share, maybe you should reevaluate your group of friends. No one likes to be taken advantage of, just like nobody appreciates a one-sided relationship.

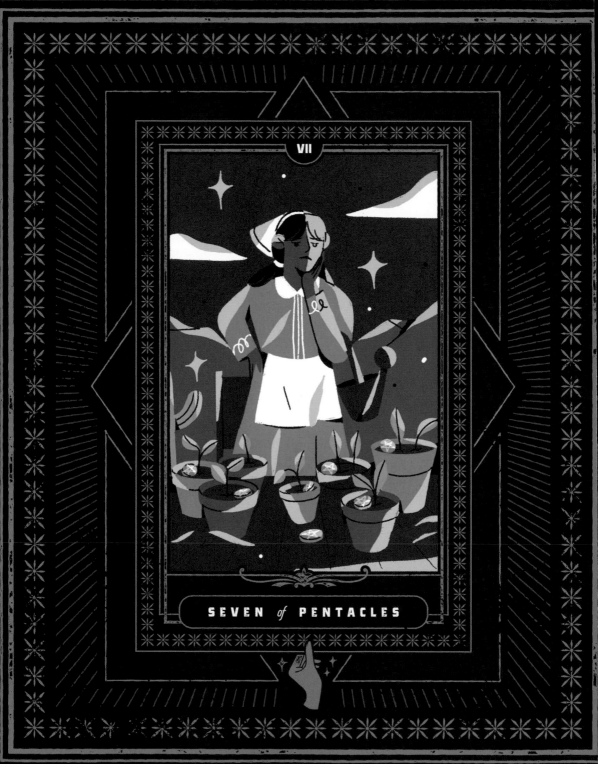

# *The* SEVEN *of* PENTACLES

## BASIC DEFINITION

The Seven of Pentacles can refer to a time in your life when you have finished a project and are now reflecting on the journey to see if it was worth it or not. Why not take a pause to check on your investment? You've put in a good amount of work so far, thoughtfully planned everything out, and now you can wait and see the rewards come in. When this card shows up in a reading, you need to be patient.

## *Reversed* BASIC DEFINITION

The Seven of Pentacles Reversed represents frustration with the time you have invested in something and potentially giving up before the project is completed. Maybe you lost faith in what you were working on, or maybe you realized that the investment would not pay off like you anticipated. Maybe you need to restructure your ideas and start anew. This card, when it shows up in a reading, makes you ask the hard questions: Is it all worthwhile? Is what I'm doing making sense for the greater good? Should I invest any more of my time working on something I am unsure about?

## TEQUILA DEFINITION

She's wanted to be a teacher ever since she was a little girl. Lining up her stuffed animals in her bedroom to teach them English and math are some of her fondest memories. Graduating from college gives her the education needed to start her professional journey; however, she has been considering going for her master's degree in education. She's sick of school right now, but she knows that if she continues her education, she will find a job faster and will get paid more. She has come so far and now she is waiting for a sign to tell her what she should do. Maybe she should take a year to think on it while subbing at some of the local schools in the area. Either way, she will be rewarded by her work invested.

## *Reversed* TEQUILA DEFINITION

Getting accepted into college is an exciting time in one's life. Starting this more responsible chapter in your life, you can't let the partying get out of control. Halfway through your freshman year and catching a lot of grief from your parents, you decide to drop out. Sure, it was a waste of time and a loss of your parents' money, but better to get out now then make the second half of the year even worse. Sometimes you have to cut your losses and rethink your life.

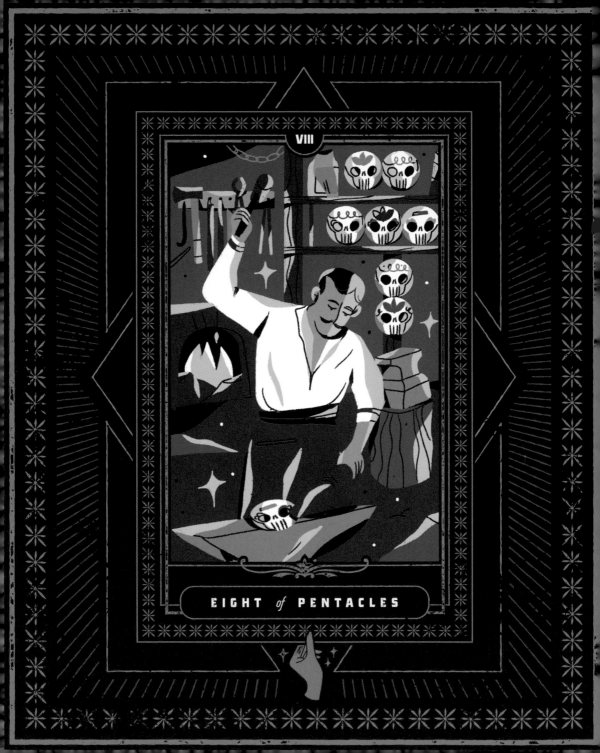

EIGHT *of* PENTACLES

# The **EIGHT** of **PENTACLES**

✳✳✳✳✳✳✳✳✳✳✳✳✳✳✳✳✳✳✳✳✳✳✳✳✳✳✳✳✳✳✳✳✳

## BASIC DEFINITION

When the Eight of Pentacles shows up in a reading, it generally means that you are hard at work to become a master at what you are passionate about. You are not taking any shortcuts. You have your head down and are doing the work. This card is all about getting your hands dirty. Your extreme focus will show everyone around you that you take your work extremely seriously, and that you will do whatever it takes to master the art of whatever is passionately driving you forward. It's a wonderful feeling to know that this is what you want to do for the rest of your life, and that you will be extremely successful at it.

## *Reversed* BASIC DEFINITION

Where the Eight of Pentacles talks about fine craftsmanship and mastery, the reversed nature of this card talks about subpar workmanship due to a number of possibilities. Maybe you are being lazy or maybe this isn't the job for you. Whatever it is, it's showing in your work. It's possible that you need to work on your self-discipline and understand that it takes time to learn a trade and master a skill. Unfortunately, we aren't born with the knowledge.

## TEQUILA DEFINITION

You took the summer bartending course mainly because your friends were taking it. You also think bartending would be a great job with your type of personality and optimism. It did come as a shock to find out that it doesn't take much to become a good mixologist, and that wasn't enough for you. Maybe you're the type of person who just needs to excel in everything you do. While your friends are joking around, you are taking this seriously. You are completely invested, and everyone can see how determined you are to get the highest of accolades in the class and land a job that will make you content and happy.

## *Reversed* TEQUILA DEFINITION

Why can't he just make a margarita the same every time? The bartender is tired. You'll give him a pass for this last one, but come on. It was barely drinkable. You aren't the best judge of character, you'll admit, but you can clearly tell that this guy does not want to be bartending right now. He's just getting by and is not enjoying his job at all. Maybe he should be honest with himself and do something different, thus allowing someone who would really like this job to step in.

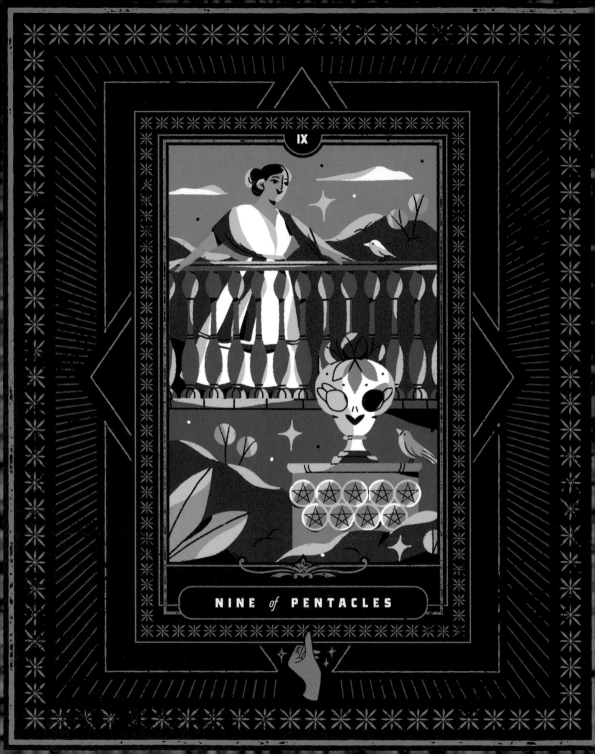

# The NINE of PENTACLES

✳✳✳✳✳✳✳✳✳✳✳✳✳✳✳✳✳✳✳✳✳✳✳✳✳✳✳✳✳✳✳✳✳✳✳

## BASIC DEFINITION

The Nine of Pentacles is a welcome card to see in any reading. It shows that you have reached a level of spiritual and material success in your life and are now able to enjoy it. The woman depicted in this card is strong and self-reliant. She is at peace within herself and does not need anyone else to make her happy; however, she will accept someone who brings their own cards to the table for a true collaborative union. The Nine of Pentacles is a card of contentment and enjoyment of a rich fulfilling life.

## TEQUILA DEFINITION

Some people feel intimidated by a strong successful man or woman. I'm referring to the individuals who don't need anyone to buy them their tequilas or dinners. These people can buy their own high-end tequila with the money that they've worked so long and hard for. They are proud of their independence and the luxury that they have created for themselves. Maybe they've invested in a top-selling tequila company before it went public and made a killing—all because they were smart enough to see the potential early on.

## Reversed BASIC DEFINITION

The Nine of Pentacles Reversed refers to someone who may be too materialistic and has a tendency to show off more than they truly have. This card can also speak to someone feeling very alone even though they are surrounded by material wealth. The Nine of Pentacles Reversed can also ask us to look into our relationship with work. It's possible you are a workaholic and maybe stressed-out because you have a fear that you will never have enough to be truly happy.

## Reversed TEQUILA DEFINITION

Some people can absolutely self-sabotage themselves by coming across as too materialistic and overindulgent. Do they even realize that other people see their gratuitous behavior as deceptive in nature? I'm sure that's why a lot of people turn down dates or drinks from people who seem too over-the-top with their appearance. Maybe they'd rather be on a date with themselves? Instead of being so concerned about your appearance and acknowledgment of how much money you are throwing around, how about just being yourself to see how that goes?

# *The*
# MYSTICAL PAIRING

*While the meaning of the Nine of Pentacles is defined as wealth and success, the time to drink it is when you're feeling the exact opposite. This cocktail only includes the finest of ingredients because you deserve nothing less.*

*Under the light of a brand-new moon your ritual can begin. Acquire four candles of different colors (yellow, orange, green, and gold work well) and write down a list of positive affirmations that resonate with you. While the candles are ablaze, say your affirmations out loud so the universe can hear you. When you've finished, take the paper and let it catch fire from each candle. Let your words of power burn away into the sky to be heard by all of your angels.*

*As the last of the smoke disappears into the night sky, raise your glass and say thank you. Thanks to all who heard you and thanks to yourself for allowing this change to happen.*

*Serve in* a collins glass

# *The* NINE OF PENTACLES COCKTAIL

1/2 LIME, CUT INTO FOUR PIECES

1 1/2 OUNCES CLASE AZUL REPOSADO TEQUILA

1/2 OUNCE CRÈME YVETTE

1/2 OUNCE AGAVE OR SIMPLE SYRUP [SEE PAGE 31]

8 FRESH MINT LEAVES, SPANKED AND RIPPED,
PLUS A SPRIG FOR GARNISH

2 OUNCES CLUB SODA, PLUS A SPLASH FOR MUDDLING

✦

*In a shaker, muddle the lime with a splash of club soda. Add ice to the shaker along with the tequila, Crème Yvette, agave or simple syrup, and mint. Shake it like you mean it! Pour into a collins glass. Finish with the club soda. Garnish with a spanked mint sprig—clap it between your hands to release the aromatics.*

# The TEN of PENTACLES

✳✳✳✳✳✳✳✳✳✳✳✳✳✳✳✳✳✳✳✳✳✳✳✳✳✳✳✳✳✳✳✳✳✳✳

## BASIC DEFINITION

The Ten of Pentacles is a card of both material and spiritual success. When this card shows up in a reading, it speaks to prosperity and security, primarily having to do with family and finances. Your generosity with your accomplishments and your devotion to your family play important roles in your life, especially when thinking about your family legacy. Thoughts of the ability to care of your children and your grandchildren after you are gone may be on your mind. The Ten of Pentacles can also mean that you are financially able to help contribute to charities and your community.

## TEQUILA DEFINITION

A wealthy restaurateur is successful enough that now their energy goes into giving back to the community and showing gratitude to the people who helped with their success. It's not just a successful enterprise but also a family business in which the children and grandchildren have active roles in running multiple restaurants. Having a family working together to reach a common goal is a wonderful definition for the Ten of Pentacles.

## *Reversed* BASIC DEFINITION

The Ten of Pentacles Reversed is a card of financial problems and misfortune. Maybe a bad financial risk was taken and now you are suffering because of it? This card asks you to reflect on what poor decisions regarding your finances you've made and instead of blaming the universe for your unfortunate luck, taking the responsibility on yourself. The Ten of Pentacles Reversed may also represent an unhealthy relationship with money. Will it ever be enough to sustain you?

## *Reversed* TEQUILA DEFINITION

You never completely trusted them, so it didn't really surprise you when you found out your employee has been stealing from you for the past six months. But still, it was a hard pill to swallow. Hiring a bad egg every so often comes with the territory. However, it affects your trust with other employees, and it also makes you worried that this will happen again.

THE MINOR ARCANA

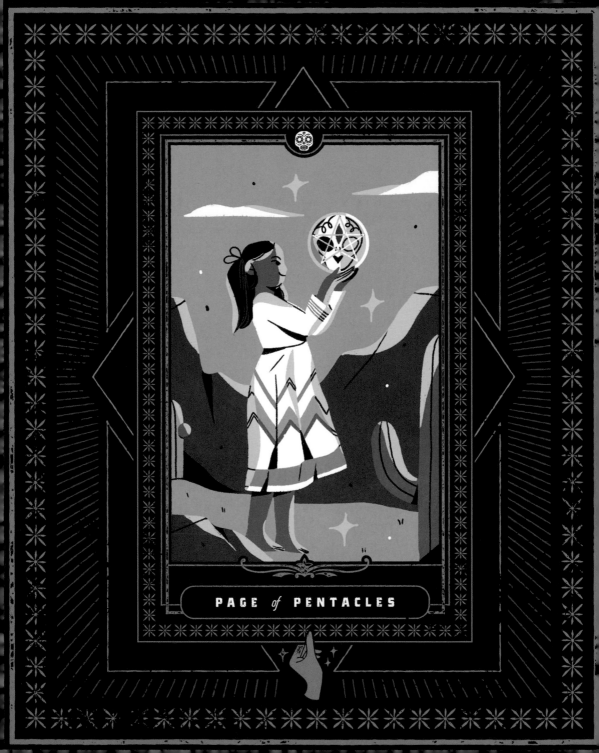

PAGE *of* PENTACLES

# The PAGE of PENTACLES

❋❋❋❋❋❋❋❋❋❋❋❋❋❋❋❋❋❋❋❋❋❋❋❋❋❋❋❋❋❋❋❋❋❋❋❋❋❋❋

## BASIC DEFINITION

A positive vibe of earthly practicalities! Like all Pages, this card brings a message; however, the grounded Page of Pentacles talks about finance, health, and home. Expect good news from work! Your employers are noticing your hard work and dependability. Even a raise or promotion can be in the works.

## TEQUILA DEFINITION

Everyone has that reliable friend who doesn't mind being the designated driver. You've asked them if they would like a drink, but they aren't so much into the party scene. They are fine being the responsible caregivers for their group of friends. The Page of Pentacles can also represent that fun local college bar where the students gather to unwind and blow off steam. It may mean that an invitation to a business or work event is on its way.

## *Reversed* BASIC DEFINITION

In reverse, this Page often brings unfortunate news in the world of work and finance. Projects are getting delayed and people you depend on are not following through. You find yourself unable to realize your plans and wonder why you are procrastinating.

## *Reversed* TEQUILA DEFINITION

Late with an RSVP, maybe you're uninterested in the overall invitation. You find yourself making excuses to get out of going places. A friend who is feeling a little reckless may need you to watch over them during an unfortunate night of one too many shots.

# *The* MYSTICAL PAIRING

*Recognize the earthly beauty of this drink before you imbibe its robust flavors. Consider the process that goes into designing the perfect cocktail. It starts with an idea, something rooted in your imagination, and it's up to you to make it real so others can now experience the work and effort that you applied. There may be some pitfalls along the way, but falling down and stumbling are part of the learning process; just don't make it part of the drinking process.*

*Enjoy this cocktail when you aspire for greater earthly things. When you are looking for the better job that will bring you financial security, let this Page of Pentacles be your messenger. Under a full moon that reminds you of a beautiful round coin, sit outside with your cocktail. Hold a silver dollar and a tiger's eye crystal in one hand and say unto the moon, "I am ready to accept good fortune," and "I am ready to receive good tidings," after every sip you take. Keep your silver dollar and crystal in your pocket for as long as you need to.*

*Serve in*   *a collins glass*

## *The*
# PAGE OF PENTACLES COCKTAIL

**1 1/2 OUNCES REPOSADO TEQUILA**

**1 OUNCE FRESH LIME JUICE**

**1/2 OUNCE GINGER AGAVE SYRUP** [RECIPE FOLLOWS]

**1 OUNCE BEET JUICE**

✦

*Fill a collins glass halfway with ice. Pour in the tequila, lime juice, and ginger agave syrup and stir. Layer in the beet juice by turning a spoon upside down inside the glass and very slowly pouring the beet juice over the spoon.*

### GINGER AGAVE SYRUP

*Combine 1 cup agave, 1 cup water, and 1 minced gingerroot in a small saucepan. Bring to a boil, then reduce to a low simmer. Let cook for about an hour. Chill overnight and keep in the refrigerator for up to two weeks.*

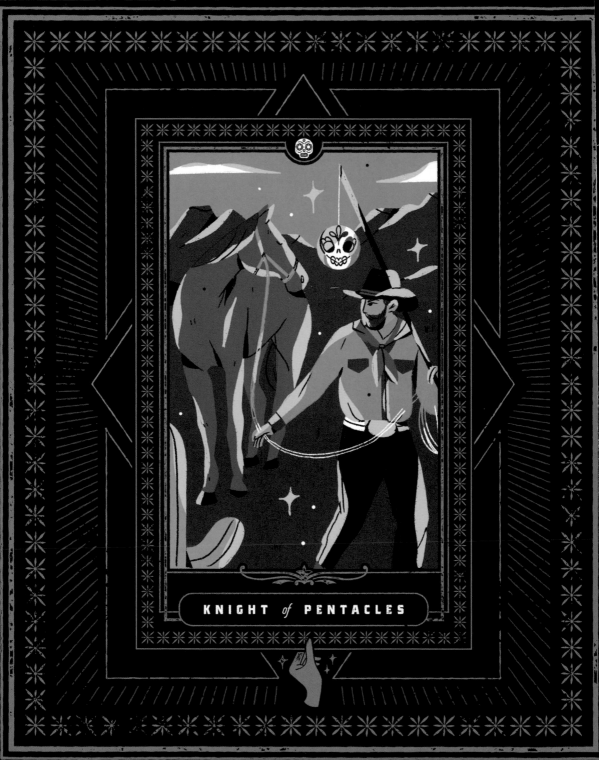

KNIGHT *of* PENTACLES

# The KNIGHT of PENTACLES

✳✳✳✳✳✳✳✳✳✳✳✳✳✳✳✳✳✳✳✳✳✳✳✳✳✳✳✳✳✳✳✳✳✳✳✳✳

## BASIC DEFINITION

The Knight of Pentacles, if referring to a person, is the young man or woman who is dedicated to doing a good job. They are very conservative and dependable and have a method and organization to their work that makes them very successful. If this card is speaking to an aspect of your personality, it may mean that now is the time to buckle down and get the work done. The way to do that is by routine and determination. The Knight of Pentacles might not be a dazzler, but they will impress you nonetheless, because they are just so likeable and organized. Everyone can use a few of these people around them to make sure the job gets done the way you expect it to.

## *Reversed* BASIC DEFINITION

Unfortunately, the Knight of Pentacles Reversed has qualities like carelessness and laziness. The reversed Knight can also represent obstacles standing in your way, not allowing you to move forward as planned. Other traits for this card would be apathy, idleness, and even possibly deception. You may be tired of your job and looking to cut corners in order to move your tedious work along. Eventually you will be called out for your lack of enthusiasm.

## TEQUILA DEFINITION

It's okay to enjoy drinking tequila. It's picking up popularity across the country now that it is being made so much better and smoother. However, being responsible is needed now more than ever. The Knight of Pentacles is all about safety and being conservative with their pours. It would be hard to imagine the Knight of Pentacles getting behind the wheel of their car while intoxicated. They would most likely call for an Uber.

## *Reversed* TEQUILA DEFINITION

The local speakeasy does no promotion or advertising, yet complains about not being successful—this is an interpretation of the Knight of Pentacles Reversed. Word of mouth just isn't working. It's easy to get bogged down in the day to day and not focus on improving your situation. Are work-related or personal problems getting in the way of your success? It's possible that the owner just doesn't care about making the bar more than what it currently is. While the bartenders and servers are not making their desired income, they question why the owner/manager doesn't aspire for more.

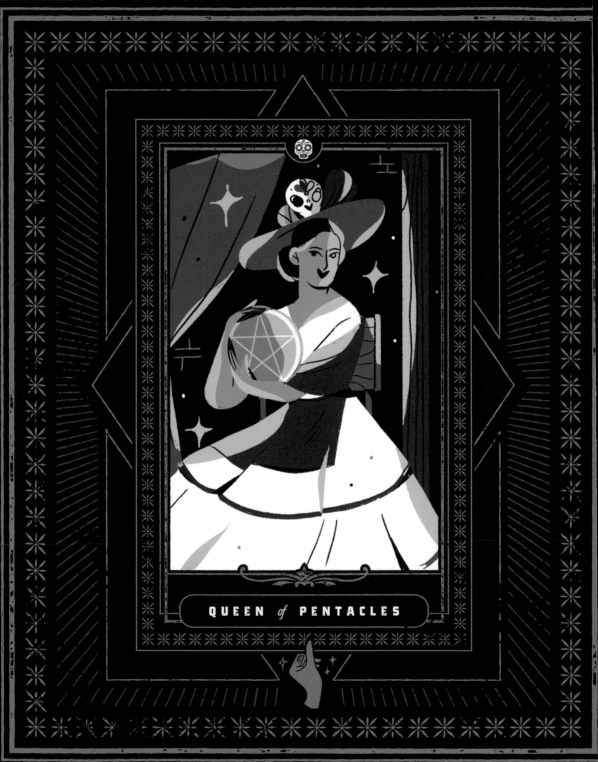

QUEEN *of* PENTACLES

# The QUEEN of PENTACLES

## BASIC DEFINITION

The Queen of Pentacles is the embodiment of what an earth mother is and should be. Someone who loves and nurtures their family ferociously, a working parent, and someone who values home and financial security are most like a Queen of Pentacles. They have a hot meal on the table, the same time each night, knowing that consistency makes everyone feel better. If this card appears in a reading and does not represent a person, it is calling on your sensual and generous side to come through for those who love and need you.

## Reversed BASIC DEFINITION

When your home life is thrown upside down and is a complete mess, you may be experiencing some Queen of Pentacles Reversed energy. The mother or father who is overprotective and smothering, or the parent who works way too much and hasn't quite found that home-work balance can also be a Queen of Pentacles Reversed. If referring to an aspect of your personality, this card may be saying that you lean a little to the materialistic and self-absorbed side of things. Relearn to embrace the qualities that made you a loving and responsible parent and spouse without overthinking the relationships and expecting too much.

## TEQUILA DEFINITION

Have you ever been waited on by somebody who makes you feel like you're right at home? The waitress lovingly calls you "Hon" or "Sweetie," not in a condescending way, but with complete affection. She's so down to earth and grounded, and the atmosphere is so comforting; the fireplace is a nice touch. It makes you feel all warm and fuzzy inside, and she makes you feel so relaxed. You instinctively know she has to be a mother, because how could she not be?

## Reversed TEQUILA DEFINITION

Your friend was always an overprotective mother, but when her kids started drinking and going to parties, she didn't know how to handle it. She thought the best course of action was to be mistrusting, and maybe she overreacted. She started grounding her kids, just to have an excuse to keep them home. She uses fear and guilt to make sure her kids always behave and stay out of trouble.

# The
# MYSTICAL PAIRING

*Amid the grind of the day to day, it's easy for us to lose our way. When we want to reconnect with the grounded nature of a happy home or need to nurture ourselves, consider this cocktail.*

*The first thing you'll want to do is prepare two spaces. First a clean space to create the elixir, the second being a comfortable space to consume it. Next, turn off all overhead fluorescent lighting and surround yourself with the soft glow of fragrant candles, not too overpowering but just the right amount to soothe your sense of smell and sight. Add soft meditative music to help create the perfect magical atmosphere and start making your cocktail.*

*When the beverage is complete, walk to your space of comfort while, along the way, sprinkling a drop or two of your drink here and there while uttering positive affirmations about what your body, house, or family needs. Sit down surrounded by pillows and more candles and quietly drink your cocktail.*

*Serve in*    *a collins glass*

# *The*
# QUEEN OF PENTACLES COCKTAIL

1/2 LIME, CUT INTO SPEARS

1 OUNCE LYCHEE PUREE

1 1/2 OUNCES PAPA'S PILAR RUM

1 DROP ROSE WATER

6 FRESH SPEARMINT LEAVES, PLUS 1 FOR GARNISH

CLUB SODA, FOR TOPPING

✦

*Muddle the lime and lychee puree in a shaker without ice. Add the rum, rose water, spearmint leaves, and ice and shake, shake, shake! Pour into a collins glass and top off with club soda. Garnish with a spanked mint leaf—clap it between your hands to bring out the aromatics.*

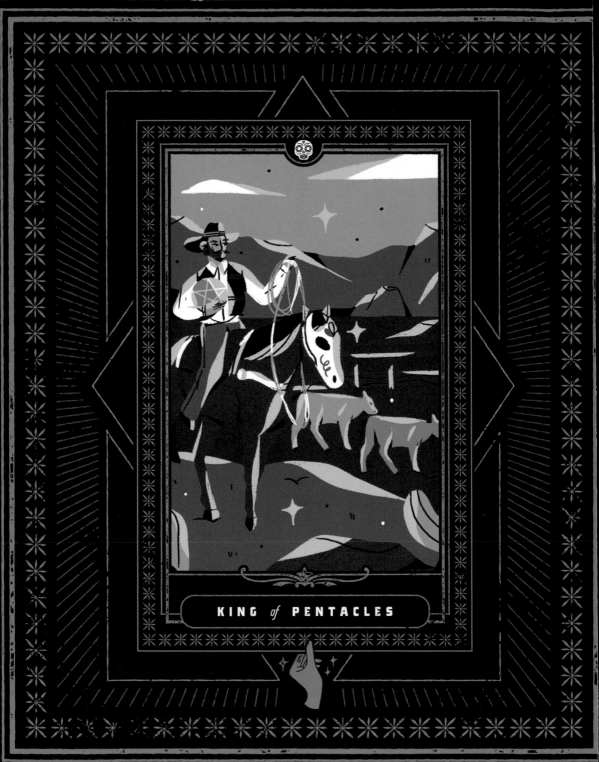

KING *of* PENTACLES

# The KING of PENTACLES

## BASIC DEFINITION

When the King of Pentacles appears in a reading, it can easily refer to a person like a father or manager who's in a position to help you out financially and has your best interests in mind. It could be a financial planner who genuinely cares about you and your family. The King of Pentacles can represent achieving comfort and security through personal growth and attaining goals. A good omen in a tarot reading, this card often means material abundance and spiritual wealth.

## *Reversed* BASIC DEFINITION

The opposite of the stable and confident King of Pentacles is an arrogant, domineering, and self-absorbed person of authority, completely obsessed with material wealth. They focus way too much on their individual status. The reversed King might instead be asking you to reflect on any poor financial investments or decisions you have made that have not turned out the way you expected. It may ask you to look at your balance between materialism and spiritualism. Are you leaning too far in one direction? The King of Pentacles Reversed can refer to someone you know who likes to be in control of your money and making decisions for you because they think they know best.

## TEQUILA DEFINITION

Who would have thought that investing in that small tequila start-up would make you some serious cash? It's true you have a sense for good business decisions; however, you've never tried anything like this before. You have always leaned on the side of practicality, security, and caution, but this seemed fun and completely unlike you. You've learned to trust your instincts and all of your friends and family come to you for financial advice, so was there ever really any doubt that this venture wouldn't be a success?

## *Reversed* TEQUILA DEFINITION

A large group of friends have decided to go out for a very nice dinner with the preconceived notion that the bill would be split evenly by everyone at the table. The night was going wonderfully, tequila was flowing, and by the time the check was placed at the end of the table, one of your friends quickly picks up the whole bill. How is that fair and/or equal? What was his motive behind it? It's funny how one gesture can do more harm than good. It replaced the flavor of tequila with an otherwise bad taste in everyone's mouth.

# ACKNOWLEDGMENTS

I would love to thank all the people who believed in this project from the beginning. I would especially like to thank my wife, Alison, and kids, Will and Charlotte, for never losing faith in my vision. Alison, thank you very much for your help and support. Love you lots!

I'd like to thank my two favorite bartenders, Ryan Loughran and Lindsey Taylor, for their magical mixology contributions. They really helped bring to life the essence of the tarot cards through their amazing bartending abilities. We paired the hell out of these cards!

I would like to thank my good friends Karen Kane, John Carleo, and Cara Milewski for their knowledge, advice, and assistance. And I cannot forget about my friends at Simon & Schuster, especially Anja Schmidt and Patrick Sullivan, for making a dream of mine come true.

I am truly blessed to have you all in my life!

# INDEX

# ABOUT *the* AUTHOR

**DAVID A. ROSS** is a medical sales representative by day and a band player/tarot card reader by night. He created a business called Tarot and Tequila, where he reads cards for people in restaurants and bars, or any place that serves tequila. His spiritual journey started twenty-five years ago when he was a tourist perusing a toy store in Santa Fe, New Mexico, where on a lark he bought a tiny tarot deck. He quickly decided that he was going to learn about tarot and form connections with other people to help them progress spiritually. Ross would love a chance to read your cards and share a spicy margarita with you. Cheers!

# ABOUT *the* CONTRIBUTORS

The son of two great bartending parents, **RYAN LOUGHRAN** started his own bartending career at the Old Bay Restaurant in New Brunswick, New Jersey, where he worked for more than a decade. He met his gorgeous wife, Colleen, there, and her love for travel and food allowed Ryan to see cocktail creativity from different perspectives. They live in Neptune, New Jersey, with their rescue dog, Roux. Colleen bartends in Asbury Park's Taka. Ryan has spent the last four happy years bartending at Teak in Red Bank.

**LINDSEY TAYLOR** has been bartending and designing cocktails for more than twenty years. The majority of her work is wild and tiki-based. Her love for the islands is what keeps her slinging drinks to this day. Lindsey has appeared on *Emeril Live* and in various magazines as a tiki specialist. Lindsey is now venturing off into her own oasis, opening R Bar in Asbury Park, New Jersey, in the winter of 2020. Drink tiki, live happy.

# ABOUT *the* ILLUSTRATOR

**CAROLINA MARTÍNEZ** is a freelance illustrator and 2D animator from Mexico City. As a freelance illustrator for the past three years, she has tried to pursue projects that reflect who she is, what she likes, and what she cares about, so that people can get to know her a little bit better through her art. Plants, women, and esotericism are never missing in what she does.